The Supreme Court and Judicial Choice

The Supreme Court and Judicial Choice

The Role of Provisional Review in a Democracy

Paul R. Dimond

Ann Arbor
The University of Michigan Press

Published in the United States of America by
The University of Michigan Press
Manufactured in the United States of America

1992 1991 1990 1989 4 3 2 1

Library of Congress Cataloging-in-Publication Data

Dimond, Paul R.
The Supreme Court and judicial choice : the role of provisional review in a democracy / Paul R. Dimond.
p. cm.
Bibliography: p.
Includes index.
ISBN 0-472-10103-X (alk. paper)
1. Judicial review—United States. 2. United States. Supreme Court. 3. Judge-made law—United States. 4. Separation of powers—United States. I. Title.
KF4575.D56 1989
347.73'26—dc19
[347.30735] 88-26709
CIP

Contents

INTRODUCTION

Judicial Choice: Confronting the Dilemma of Judicial Review in a Democracy

The independent judiciary has always played a role in the development of law within the constitutional system of representative democracy in the United States. In elaborating the common law over time, interpreting statutes, and articulating the meaning of the Constitution, judges resolve cases or controversies that other parties bring before the courts. Although prior precedent, judicial tradition, and the relevant legal texts provide guidance, laws enacted by democratically elected legislatures and constitutional provisions adopted by the people do not always give a specific answer to the issues raised in these cases. Instead, judges often are forced to make hard choices. Inevitably, courts produce new law through this process of adjudication.[1]

In the context of common law development and statutory interpretation, such judicial lawmaking can be understood as an integral part of an ongoing dialogue with the people over what rules should govern our conduct and what personal rights should limit the power of government. Court rulings merely posit a point of view that the people are free to reject, to modify, or to codify by enacting statutes through their elected representatives in the legislature. In the context of constitutional adjudication, however, the Supreme Court's lawmaking role does not seem to fit so easily within the framework of majority rule in our representative democracy. When the Court articulates its view of the meaning of the Constitution, its word is commonly regarded as final, subject to rejection or modification only through the cumbersome and antimajoritarian process of constitutional amendment, which requires a proposal supported by two-thirds of the House and Senate and ratified by three-fourths of the several states.

The Court's voice in constitutional cases takes on added weight for another reason as well. Our Constitution forms a government of limited powers, with an array of checks and balances. The powers of government are both enumerated in and restricted by the Constitution. In declaring acts of Congress, the President, or the states unconstitutional, the Court of course invalidates the governmental action. But, in upholding acts of the Congress, the President, or the states, the Court determines that the government has acted properly within the bounds of its limited power.

The full weight and prestige of the Court may thereby be placed behind the policy choice made by the government.[2] In constitutional cases, therefore, the Court's word is more than final: it appears to be authoritative. As a result, the Court's voice often proves determinative for generations to come.[3]

The Court, itself, has recognized this awesome lawmaking power by holding that its precedents in constitutional cases should not be given as much weight as in cases of statutory interpretation, precisely because it is so difficult for the people to alter the Court's constitutional judgments.[4] After all, if the people can't modify the Court's constitutional rulings by having their elected representatives enact legislation, at least the Court itself has to be able to modify, to change or to reverse its prior rulings in order to correct its own errors[5] or to meet circumstances unforeseen at the time of initial judicial ruling.*

This power of lawmaking by unelected Justices in constitutional cases, however, has long been a source of controversy among judicial pundits and politicians because it seems so inconsistent with the basic tenet of majority rule in a representative democracy. Most recently, this issue dominated the confirmation hearings and ultimate rejection by the Senate of President Reagan's nomination of Robert Bork as an Associate Justice of the United States Supreme Court. Ever since his initial cam-

*The Supreme Court is not always this straightforward in acknowledging its lawmaking power when interpreting the Constitution. The Court often presents (or the public wants to see) a different face, that of a messenger merely delivering the message clearly revealed by the Constitution itself to anyone conscientious enough to look carefully. The Court's own creative role in interpreting the Constitution, however, has increasingly emerged. For example, the Court has simply given up trying to ground its long-standing protection of the individual's right to relocate and move freely about the country in any particular provision in the Constitution; the right to travel has simply been posited by the Court, and accepted by the people, as a fundamental personal right, whatever its particular source. *Compare* Crandall v. Nevada, 6 Wall. 35, 44 (1868) *with* United States v. Guest, 383 U.S. 745, 757–58 (1966), and Shapiro v. Thompson, 394 U.S. 618, 630 (1969). Even a conservative Justice like John Harlan came to describe the "constitutional inquiry" in personal rights cases in similarly open-ended terms: whether the governmental action "infringes the due process clause . . . because [it] violates basic values implicit in the concept of ordered liberty." Griswold v. Connecticut, 381 U.S. 479, 499 (1965). Even if the Constitution authorizes the Court to undertake this "inquiry," it does not provide a ready answer to such a general question for any Justice. As Justice Brennan recently recognized in describing the "unique interpretive role of the Supreme Court with respect to the Constitution," the Court's rulings must therefore "be subject to revision over time, or the Constitution falls captive . . . to the anachronistic views of long-gone generations." Judicial review, inevitably, is an "evolutionary process," which Justice Brennan proclaimed the "true interpretive genius of the text" of the Constitution. Brennan Speech, *reprinted in* FEDERALIST SOCIETY, THE GREAT DEBATE: INTERPRETING OUR WRITTEN CONSTITUTION 24 (1986).

paigns, President Reagan has repeatedly bashed the Warren and Burger Courts for judicial activism. In constitutional cases, he has argued that unelected Justices should not make up their own law but should only enforce the law provided by the people in the Constitution. Under this idyllic vision, the Court would merely declare the specific answers to be found by any strict constructionist conscientious enough to look at the text and framing of the Constitution. With the retirement of Justice Powell, President Reagan appeared to have the opportunity to place a Justice on the Court who might be able to form a new majority to implement the President's judicial philosophy. President Reagan claimed that Robert Bork, if confirmed by the Senate, would stand by those who enforce only the rules of law clearly and unequivocally embodied in the Constitution by the framers.[6]

As the confirmation hearings unfolded, however, Judge Bork was hoist on the President's petard. On many important constitutional issues (e.g., the Court's expansive reading of congressional power under the commerce clause, broad interpretation of the meaning of equal protection and of due process in the school segregation cases, enforcement of free speech protection far beyond political expression and active refereeing of separation of power disputes between Congress and the President), Bork went out of his way to show that he was no neoconservative judicial radical bent on overturning the Court's prior precedents in these areas. Although he occasionally suggested that such rulings had some support in the framing and text of the Constitution, he never claimed that they were compelled by the original intention. Bork conceded, albeit grudgingly at times, that he was willing to live with the judicial law made in the past in such cases, whether or not the framing and text of the Constitution required the interpretive choice when the issues first arose before the Court.[7]

Why then, the Senators pressed, did Bork choose to question Court rulings that gave a similarly broad interpretation of personal autonomy and privacy rights under a substantive reading of the due process clause (or an expansive reading of the wall of separation between church and state under the first amendment or broad procedural protections for criminal defendants under the fourth through sixth amendments or narrow protection of state sovereignty from congressional regulation)?[8] Although Bork responded by inveighing against unelected judges making law and by giving a treatise on the limits of *stare decisis* in constitutional cases,[9] the Senate ultimately rejected his answer by a vote of 9 to 5 in the Judiciary Committee and 58 to 42 on the Senate floor.

In truth, the Bork hearings confirmed that the Constitution has not, does not, and can not provide a single answer to every issue that is brought before the Court. Witnessing the inevitability of judicial choice in interpreting the Constitution so starkly revealed before the Judiciary Committee, the Senate finally rejected Robert Bork because a majority of the

Senators were unwilling to trust *his* choice of which current doctrines he might accept and which he might question. If President Reagan nominated Bork to challenge the broad thrust of the Modern Court's making of law in interpreting the Constitution, the Senate responded by defending the Court's process of lawmaking within the context of constitutional adjudication, if not each of its policy choices.

The Bork confirmation hearings, therefore, confronted the fundamental tension of judicial review in a democracy: if the Constitution in many cases authorizes a range of choices rather than providing a single answer, how does the inevitable process of unelected Justices with life tenure making constitutional law fit with the basic premise of majority rule in a representative democracy? The Senate answered by participating in this process of judicial choice in constitutional adjudication by rejecting the President's nomination on the merits of Robert Bork's judicial philosophy, not on his unquestioned qualifications.[10]

This book explores a new approach to the basic issue of judicial choice by asking whether there is any way under the Constitution as written to understand judicial rulings in constitutional cases as *provisional* rather than *final*. The burden of this book is to demonstrate that, in important respects, judicial choices in interpreting the Constitution can be understood not as final judgments forever binding on the people but as provisional rulings that initiate an ongoing dialogue with the people.

This concept of the provisional nature of judicial review is not revolutionary. It builds upon the evolutionary process through which constitutional law has changed over time. Where the text and framing of the Constitution provide no clear answer to the issues presented, the Court inevitably posits a point of view over the meaning of the Constitution in deciding such hard cases. Over time, we the people respond to the Court's interpretation, either by acquiescing in the ruling or by framing a different understanding, whether by legislation, argument before the Court or in other public arenas, our conduct, the appointment of new Justices, or constitutional amendment. The Court, in turn, *is* influenced by this process and, over the generations, moves to distinguish, to modify, or to reverse its prior interpretation or simply accepts the supplanting understanding. Although the outcome of this dialogue over the meaning of the Constitution is not as easily controlled by the people through their elected representatives, it does share many of the democratic characteristics of statutory interpretation and the elaboration of common law.

To stimulate further thinking on judicial review as an ongoing dialogue between the Court and the people, this book will explore *one* reading of the structure of the Constitution under which (*a*) a surprising variety of Supreme Court rulings in constitutional cases would be subject to modification, rejection, or approval by *ordinary* legislation duly enacted by the people's representatives in Congress and (*b*) a surprisingly narrow category of judgments would be subject to revision *only* by a process of public debate and either judicial evolution or constitutional amendment. This theory is therefore called *provisional review*.

The term *theory* of judicial review has become somewhat confusing because constitutional scholars often support their normative claims of how the Court *should* act with their descriptions of how the Court *does* act. Perhaps, this is understandable in a discipline such as law, where the practitioners are trained to be advocates. In contrast, this book offers provisional review neither as a certain prescription for how the Court should act, nor as a precise description of how the Court does act. Instead, provisional review offers a new way of thinking about how the Court has sometimes acted in the past and could act in the future to protect the interests of the individual and of the minority under our Constitution as written *consistent* with majority rule in a representative democracy. Provisional review provides a different lens through which to see how the Court may interact with the people over time in interpreting the Constitution. When viewed from this perspective, judicial choice in constitutional cases may then be seen more clearly as an integral part of the lawmaking process through which we the people govern ourselves by engaging in a national dialogue over the meaning of the Constitution. In positing a point of view, the Court's rulings can be understood as beginning rather than ending this process of interpretation.

Traditional Theories of Judicial Review

Before exploring the underpinnings and implications of provisional review, it may be helpful to examine how alternative theories of judicial review wrestle with the dilemma of judicial choice in a democracy. Constitutional theories fall into two main camps—interpretivism, which claims that judges should decide constitutional issues solely by discovering norms found in the Constitution; and noninterpretivism, which argues that the Justices must often look beyond the Constitution for principles to decide constitutional cases that come before the Court.[11]

Interpretivism

Interpretivism starts with the premise that the people have passed a binding social contract, the Constitution, whose provisions limit the discretion of each succeeding majority's elected legislature to enact laws. An independent judiciary appointed for life then acts as the guardian with final authority to interpret the Constitution. This Supreme Court resolves cases and controversies between individual citizens and the majority will by enforcing the previously adopted constitutional restrictions on the current elected lawmakers. In 1803 in the *Marbury* case, Chief Justice John Marshall first asserted this power of final judicial review for the Court. He ruled that Congress acted unconstitutionally in seeking to expand the original jurisdiction of the Supreme Court beyond that provided in section 3 of Article III of the Constitution: "It is emphatically the province and the duty of the judicial department to say what the law is. . . . So if a [congressional act] be in opposition to the constitution, . . . [it] is void. . . . [That is] the very foundation of all written constitutions."[12]

Under the interpretivist theory of judicial review, the Court's role is limited to ascertaining what restrictions the Constitution imposes, with any ambiguities in the meaning of the text resolved by reference to the framers' intent, and then measuring whether current acts exceed those bounds. Given the generality of much of the Constitution's text, the focus in controversial cases often turns to the framers' intent.[13] Under this approach any judicially enforced constitutional limitations on majority rule are final and can be altered only by amending the Constitution or through the Court's own reinterpretation of the document itself. It is the Supreme Court's function to say what the Constitution means. The ends of democracy are said to be served because unelected Justices do not make up their own law but merely seek out and apply the original intentions of the framers who promulgated the constitutional provisions in question, which have been ratified by the people's representatives in the state legislatures.[14]

Despite its surface allure, this theory of judicial review suffers from several shortcomings and, finally, fails even to confront the dilemma of judicial choice. *First,* interpretivism, even in theory, is a curiously undemocratic notion. To the extent that the framers intended to impose restrictions on the discretion of future legislatures, the interpretivist theory requires that the dead hand from the past limits the ability of the people to respond to today's needs and to plan for tomorrow's imperatives through legislation. Moreover, the historic fact is that representatives elected by a small minority of the people framed and ratified the Constitution and most of its amendments; until well into the twentieth century, suffrage was basically limited to a relatively few, privileged white males. The vast majority of the people, therefore, never had the opportunity to consent to the Constitution as any kind of social contract binding on themselves, let alone future generations.

Second, in actual operation, the interpretivist theory relies on future Justices to divine what framers from bygone eras intended to impose as restrictions. For several reasons, this is no mean task, even for the most conscientious judge. Committees bent on political compromise drafted the various constitutional provisions, many in as general a phrasing as possible in order to avoid political controversy. Not surprisingly, the legislative history of the Constitutional Convention and of congressional debates on amendments proposed thereafter usually does not provide a specific code meaning for the general text. The state conventions and legislatures that ratified the Constitution and its amendments may have been comprised of even more diverse understandings of what restrictions were intended. The recorded materials from these ratification proceedings are even less informative: they are skimpy, opaque, and largely rhetorical. When the interpretivist Justice then seeks to find a specific answer for a case before the Court today from the framers in the past, silence may be the only greeting: the historic record often does not reveal whether the framers ever even considered, let alone resolved, the particular issue for decision.[15] Finally, today's Justice must inevitably look for such answers from the past through a lens that has been focused by a subsequent history that the framers could not have foreseen.[16]

Although there may be some Herculean judge who can find the right answer to precisely what the framers intended in each case, such difficulties of interpretation add a practical element to skepticism about the fit between interpretivism and the principles of representative democracy.

Third, neither the Supreme Court nor its critics have adhered on any principled basis to interpretivism over the two-hundred-year history of the Constitution and the Court. Indeed, this theory of judicial review has been supported or attacked by political and judicial conservatives or liberals at various times depending on the *content* of the Court's decisions, without regard to whether the Court claimed that the framers intended one result or another. In recent years, for example, conservatives have opposed the "substantive" due process rulings of the Warren and Burger Courts. Without claiming specific annointment by the framers, these decisions proclaim the individual's interest in conscience, privacy, personal autonomy, family, and the decisions on whether to bear or to beget a child against diverse forms of state regulation.[17] Conservatives of our time trumpet the interpretivist theory of judicial review in claiming that the framers of the fourteenth amendment never intended such restrictions on state sovereignty. They decry such decisions as blatant judicial lawmaking.[18]

Lest any liberal be too sanguine about the history of the Supreme Court in acting as an unelected creator and guardian of such supposedly fundamental personal rights under a substantive reading of the due process clause, it is worth remembering that the Supreme Court after the *Marbury* case in 1803 did not declare another act of Congress unconstitutional until 1857 in the infamous *Dred Scott* decision.[19] There the Court held, on the most specious grounds, that the framers could not have contemplated that any black, whether slave or free, could be a citizen of the United States with any right to sue in the federal courts. Not content with claiming that the framers intended that no black person could invoke the jurisdiction of federal courts, the Court proceeded gratuitously to reach the merits of the controversy. The Court held Congress's attempt in the Missouri Compromise to grapple with the divisive issue of slavery unconstitutional: as the Justices viewed Dred Scott only as an enslaved chattel, the Court ruled that the due process clause of the fifth amendment drained Congress of power to deprive the purported owner of this "property." Progressives and moderates of the time understandably railed against the decision, while conservative slaveholders rejoiced. It took a civil war and a constitutional amendment to reverse the Court's interpretation.

Two generations later, from 1905 through 1937, another conservative Court also interpreted the due process clauses substantively to proclaim a constitutional liberty of contract. These decisions were made, however, without *any* regard for what the framers did or did not intend. The Court supervised and often rejected progressive attempts by the states and the Congress to regulate the abuses of the industrial workplace and to promote the national economy or the general welfare.[20] In dissenting from the Court's imposition of such laissez-faire political doctrines, Justice Holmes tartly noted that the "Constitution is not intended to embody a particular economic theory." The fourteenth amendment did not enact "Mr. Herbert Spencer's Social Statics."[21] Not surprisingly, conservative economic interests hailed the Court, while liberals argued that a majority of the Justices merely substituted their personal policy preferences without regard to the framers' intent for the laws duly enacted by the people's representatives in Congress and the state legislatures. It took a depression, the New Deal, Roosevelt's threat to pack the Court, a new breed of criticism known as "legal realism," and the continued onslaught of all variety of federal and state regulatory legislation before a majority of the Justices finally ceased reviewing the substance of such economic and social welfare laws under the due process clauses.[22]

Given this shifting history of Supreme Court review and criticism, people should be as skeptical of conservative charges today that the Court should enforce only the framers' original intent as of liberal claims that the Court may always be trusted, today and tomorrow, to act as the guardian of fundamental individual rights by interpreting the due process clauses substantively. With the retirement of Justice Powell, President Reagan's vow to appoint Justices to the Court to enforce his own view of the policies intended by the framers, and the continuing concerns in the Senate and the nation over the impact a shift in the balance on the Court may have on future decisions for generations to come,[23] it is especially appropriate to examine the basic premises of this interpretivist approach to judicial review.

Imagine the chagrin of liberals today who defend the Supreme Court as the final arbiter of the meaning of the Constitution if a future Court were to declare, for example, that (*a*) the fetus is a person whose life must be absolutely protected under all circumstances by the due process clauses, (*b*) that the corporation and the individual have vested property and liberty of contract interests under the due process clauses that cannot be regulated by Congress or the states unless the regulation is deemed reasonable by the Court itself, and (*c*) that states as sovereign entities are free to declare a state religion because the fourteenth amendment does *not* incorporate any part of the first amendment.[24] Such scenarios should make even the staunchest defenders of the Supreme Court as the final authority on the meaning of the Constitution explore the basic institutional question from the philosopher's perspective, a veil of ignorance: neither conservatives nor liberals can know whether a majority of Justices on the Court will act in the decades ahead out of one particular mindset or another about what exactly the framers intended.

Fourth, whatever the merits of the dispute as to whether conservatives or liberals of one era or another have properly found the framers' true intent, the interpretivist theory of final judicial review in our democracy fails to confront the dilemma of judicial choice: in many cases, the constitutional text and framers' intent authorize a range of choices on the constitutional limits intended to be imposed on future generations. Almost all constitutional pundits recognize that some provisions of the Constitution are this general.[25] Even the most detailed examination of the historical record demonstrates that these open-ended provisions authorize a range of meanings as to the restrictions to be placed on future generations of legislatures.[26]

Such provisions cannot dictate a particular answer to every question in every case for the conscientious judge seeking to divine the intended constitutional limits on legislative discretion. Instead, they authorize a range of choices. In these circumstances, the courts cannot rely on a specific policy choice adopted by the framers in the past in determining whether a current legislature has enacted a law in contravention of the Constitution. Although prior precedents and judicial traditions provide some guidance, each Justice *must* make his or her own choice about the meaning of the Constitution in such cases.[27] In so doing, the Court inevitably posits new law as new doctrines emerge, evolve, and develop or are eroded and replaced over time through this process of constitutional adjudication. In the face of this dilemma of judicial choice among a range of alternatives, the allure of interpretivism as any kind of democratic theory of judicial review vanishes. In such cases, unelected Justices—and not the framers—must make the choice of whether, when, and how to restrict the people's representative legislatures.

To demonstrate the inevitability of judicial choice in interpreting the meaning of such open-ended provisions, chapter 1 explores the fourteenth amendment, with a focus on the equal protection clause. Chapter 1 examines the framers' intent, the text and framing of the amendment, and its relationship to the constitutional structure. The Court's interpretations of the fourteenth amendment are evaluated in the two most significant race cases, first in *Plessy v. Ferguson,*[28] upholding state-mandated segregation in 1896, and then in *Brown v. Board of Education,*[29] overturning this reading in 1954. This case study provides a dramatic example of how Justices must make their own choice about the specific meaning of important constitutional provisions, here of the equal protection clause.[30] The

Constitution in its generality does not provide a specific answer but authorizes a range of choices, even in articulating and applying a relatively straightforward nondiscrimination principle.[31]

Noninterpretivism

Fundamental Value Review

This unavoidable fact of judicial choice in interpreting the meaning of the fourteenth amendment led Alexander Bickel, perhaps the leading scholar of the Supreme Court in the past thirty years, to search beyond the four corners of the Constitution for the answer to the question, what fundamental values should the Court articulate for the nation?[32] From the outset, however, Bickel attempted to find such fundamental values outside the personal preferences of the Justices.[33] He also promoted an array of procedural devices to help prevent the Court from making too many decisions on the merits of such policy choices.[34] Near the end of his life, as he became increasingly troubled by the substance and sources of the personal rights rulings of the Warren and then the Burger Court, Bickel began to express his disenchantment with the legitimacy of such a judicial search for fundamental values in a nation committed by its Constitution to democratic rule.[35] At the end of this lifetime search, the nagging doubt grew that judges make law by choosing which values are deemed fundamental.[36]

Representation-Reinforcing Review

John Hart Ely responded by suggesting that Bickel's odyssey had been doomed from the beginning because he searched for an answer to the wrong question.[37] Ely argues that the Court's role is not to find right answers to substantive policy choices which he claims are better left for decision by the people through the democratic process.[38] Nevertheless, Ely does recognize that the text of the Constitution (e.g., the privileges or immunities clause of the fourteenth amendment) authorizes the Court to review the policy choices of state legislatures.[39] But he suggests that the Court should choose not to review any such substantive judgments until "a principled approach to judicial enforcement of [such] open-ended provisions [can] be developed [that] is consistent with the Nation's commitment to representative democracy."[40] Thus, Ely would interpret the due process clauses and the Bill of Rights restrictively as applying only to fair procedures and keeping the channels of political change open.[41] He would limit equal protection review to assuring that electoral processes are inclusive and fair (e.g., one person, one vote) and that no majority "in-group" (e.g., whites) in control of ostensibly democratic institutions systematically discriminates against a minority "out-group" (e.g., blacks) by reason of prejudice.[42]

For Ely, the Court's power of judicial review should be limited to enforcing such representation-reinforcing values in order to assure that the political process is genuinely democratic, regardless of the substantive outcome of any particular policy choice made by the people's duly elected representatives.[43] Although this process-oriented approach to judicial review seems consistent with democratic theory, it does make a dead letter of important provisions of the Constitution. It thereby selectively deprives the Court of its ability to lead the nation in a dialogue about more substantive values that we may hold as dear under the Constitution. Ely frankly concedes that he rejects judicial review of the merits of any such substantive value choices precisely because he can find no way to square such substantive review with the democratic process.[44]

Toward a New Theory of Judicial Review: Provisional Review

None of these theories of judicial review has been able to resolve adequately the dilemma of judicial choice in a democracy *if* the Supreme Court's word is understood as *final*. The burden of this book is to explore whether a more workable understanding of the dynamics of judicial review can be developed if the Supreme Court's decisions are not viewed as final and binding in all circumstances, but rather as *provisional* in some cases. At a minimum, the dilemma of judicial choice in a representative democracy is substantially reduced if not entirely eliminated if the people's elected representatives retain some power to legislate a different result from that reached by the Court. Such a provisional approach may seem a radical departure from traditional notions of judicial supremacy when stated so boldly. It does, however, have roots in the history of the Court, the text and structure of the Constitution, the federal nature of our nation, and the Court's own jurisprudence.

Harry Wellington and Terry Sandalow have begun to hint at such a provisional approach. In their writing, they observe that the Court's interpretations may not, in fact, be final and binding in all cases.[45] First, through the process of constitutional amendment, the people have overturned several judicial rulings.[46] Second, subsequent Courts have in many other instances eroded, distinguished, ignored, or directly overruled previous rulings in response to their new understandings of the right answers or of the proper role of the Court, to the appointment of new Justices, and to the reactions of the people and the political process over time.[47] Finally, in interpreting the meaning of statutes to avoid constitutional confrontation, the Court often enters into a dialogue with Congress over the meaning of the Constitution.[48] From this perspective, the Court's decisions may be seen as more like provisional judgments ultimately subject to modification or rejection through a variety of means, including the concerted will of the people over time.[49]

Wellington counsels, "We the people consent [to judicial review] . . . because we believe that, in one fashion or another, we have adequate control over the content of the law that governs us."[50] Such a vision of the Court as the initiator of a dialogue with the people over the meaning of the Constitution—and not as the final arbiter—certainly makes judicial review more consistent with the principle of majority rule in a representative democracy.[51]

Yet this understanding of how the Court's decisions are not always final and binding when viewed across generations is somewhat misleading. Most rulings by the Court are perceived as final at any given time; they don't seem to be subject to revision by simple legislation. Equally troublesome, this retrospective view does not offer any insight into which types of decisions should be viewed as provisional and which, if any, should be understood as final unless revised by a subsequent amendment to the Constitution. Finally, the approach offers little insight into how, if at all, the Court should act under the Constitution to respond to the people's will or to shape the ongoing dialogue over the meaning of the Constitution.

Jesse Choper's analysis of federalism cases in the context of our national political process begins to provide a part of the framework necessary to develop a more coherent view of provisional review.[52] In these cases the Court resolves disputes, for example, between perceived federal interests and conflicting state practices. The Court has little reason to trust the self-interested substantive policy choice enacted by the state because the federal interests affected were not represented in the state's legislative process. In many of these cases, the Court must resolve the federal-state conflict in the first instance without the benefit of any guidance from Congress. In such cases, the Court must therefore act much as a common law court positing a substantive policy choice, both in articulating the federal interest and in choosing whether it should prevail as against the conflicting state policy. Congress, in which the people of all of the states are represented, then may exercise its enumerated powers under Article I of the Constitution to reach a different result—to enlarge or to eliminate the federal interest asserted or ignored by the Court, to ratify or to alter the balance as against state policy, or simply to authorize each of the states to come up with its own solution if Congress thinks that makes more sense.

Chapter 2 therefore begins by exploring these federalism cases in order to understand the basic structure of the Constitution in which federal law is generally understood as supreme over state law. In these cases, the Court operates not as the final arbiter but as the available neutral forum in which to referee federal-state disputes in the first instance; and the Court's rulings are subject to revision by Congress exercising its enumerated powers.

Choper's understanding of this provisional form of judicial review under our national political process is limited to federalism cases and does not extend to cases involving individual rights under the Constitution.[53] The text of section 1 of the fourteenth amendment and its relationship to the structure of the entire Constitution, however, *do* provide a similar framework for judicial review of individual rights cases on a provisional basis. By its own terms, the fourteenth amendment's first section specifically protects individuals only against *state* actions that "abridge the privileges or immunities of citizens of the United States," "deprive any person of life, liberty or property without due process of law," or "deny to any person the equal protection of the laws." As a result, section 1 of the fourteenth amendment does not restrict federal power in the slightest.

Article I of the Constitution, moreover, has been interpreted to vest Congress with the power necessary to declare national rights against contrary claims of state sovereignty. In particular, section 8 of article I enumerates a variety of congressional powers that have been held sufficient to regulate the conduct of the people, otherwise to provide for the general welfare, and to declare national rights and wrongs. Although the Court has occasionally expressed doubts about the scope of this national lawmaking power, the Supreme Court has generally chosen to interpret the enumerated powers of Congress as plenary except insofar as limited by *other* provisions of the Constitution,[54] most importantly the Bill of Rights.[55]

Provisional review under the fourteenth amendment therefore builds on the bedrock of our constitutional structure—the supremacy of federal over state law that Chief Justice Marshall proclaimed 170 years ago in the *McCulloch, Gibbons,* and *Hunter's Lessee* cases in upholding federal statutes *and* Supreme Court rulings against conflicting claims of state sovereignty.[56] Although Chief Justice Marshall recognized in these cases that the structure of the Constitution as a whole might place *some* limits on the supremacy of federal over conflicting state law,[57] he made the choice that the Court should generally respect the judgment of Congress on the issue of federal versus state authority because "[i]n the legislature of the Union alone are [the people of the states] all represented. The legislature of the Union alone, therefore, can be trusted by the people with the power of controlling measures which concern all, in the confidence that it will not be abused."[58] Except for a few periods of aberration, the Court has since chosen to uphold federal law against conflicting claims of state sovereignty.[59] If the people wish to allocate more or less legislative power to the states or to Congress in our federal system, they remain free to do so through appropriate national legislation so long as the Court chooses *not* to hamstring Congress in the name of the Constitution.

Under provisional review, the states must continue to respect the Court's interpretation of the fourteenth amendment until constitutionally altered, modified, or voided by an act of Congress, a subsequent Court ruling, or a constitutional amendment. For example, as the Court ruled in the *Cooper* case in an opinion signed by *each* of the nine Justices,[60] the Governor of Arkansas was bound by the supremacy clause to respect the Court's prior holding that state-mandated segregation of the public schools violates the equal protection clauses.[61] After all, as the Supreme Court later observed, "the very purpose" of Reconstruction era constitutional amendments, civil rights laws, and expansions of federal court jurisdiction was "to interpose the federal courts between the States and the people, as guardians of the people's federal rights" in the first instance.[62]

To understand better how this provisional form of judicial review operates, assume that the Court chooses to hold that a particular state action (e.g., a state law restricting a person's choice to bear or to beget a child) "abridges the privileges or immunities of citizens of the United States."[63] Such an interpretation of section 1 of the fourteenth amendment would bind the States, but it would not restrict (because section 1 of the fourteenth amendment does not restrict) the Congress from enacting subsequent legislation within its enumerated powers under article I enforcing, modifying, revising, or even rejecting the Court's policy choice. The Court's decision would, of course, continue to bind the states until modified by the Court itself or supplanted by a constitutional act of Congress. In this sense, the Court's interpretations of the fourteenth amendment as against the states would initiate a national dialogue with the people through their elected representatives in Congress over what are the individual's fundamental national rights under our Constitution. Chapter 2 concludes by exploring this structure for understanding both the Court's initial review of state substantive value choices under section 1 of the fourteenth amendment and congressional power to enact a different result under article I.

Chapter 3 will then explore the nature of the *limits* that the Constitution *does* place on this legislative power of Congress, primarily through the Bill of Rights. The Bill of Rights, in addition to protecting the individual in a variety of ways from unfair treatment at the hands of the federal government in civil or criminal proceedings, protects only a relatively few substantive values from federal encroachment in certain circumstances. The first amendment prohibits Congress from making a law respecting an establishment of religion, or prohibiting the free exercise thereof. The second amendment, at least with respect to state militia, prohibits the federal government from infringing on the people's right to keep and bear arms. The third amendment prohibits the federal government from quartering troops in any house in time of peace except with the owner's consent. The fourth amendment protects people, their homes, papers, and personal effects against unreasonable searches and seizures. The fifth amendment prohibits the federal government from taking private property except for public use and then only with just compensation. And the eighth amendment prohibits infliction of cruel and unusual punishment.

To the extent that the Court chooses to interpret these substantive values as binding, Congress may *not* abridge the Court's judgments, either directly by statute or indirectly by seeking to delegate authority to other federal agencies or to the states. On these substantive values the Court's interpretation, like that in *Marbury*,[64] is *not* subject to revision by congressional legislation, although it may be subject to erosion or development as future Courts respond to the people's understanding of the meaning of such provisions.

The more important point is that these few substantive values are relatively narrow in scope when compared, for example, to the more general and open-ended privileges or immunities of citizens of the United States that the Court may choose to protect against state interference under the fourteenth amendment. Thus, broad areas of fourteenth amendment protection are *not* covered by the Bill of Rights *if* the Court chooses to interpret the fifth amendment's due process clause as limited to procedural rights rather than protecting unspecified substantive values. Congress may legislate different substantive results for the nation in these areas.

In so doing, the Congress will exercise its enumerated powers under article I, and the Court engages in judicial review of such legislation in the traditional sense as a final arbiter under *Marbury*. Unless the Bill of Rights limits congressional power, however, there is *no* constitutional violation for the Court to declare.[65] Thus, the very structure of the Constitution invites this form of provisional review of what constitute national substantive rights *not* specified in the Bill of Rights. In these matters of state authority versus federal right, the structure of the Constitution authorizes the Court to recognize the national lawmaking power of Congress as supreme, except where other provisions such as the Bill of Rights may be interpreted as restricting the otherwise plenary congressional power.

Under this reading of the structure of the Constitution, however, the Bill of Rights may still be interpreted as imposing important limits on the *manner* by which Congress decides to legislate different substantive results. Chapter 3 explores the potential extent and sensitivity of this *process*-oriented review of national legislation that is authorized by this understanding of the basic thrust of the Bill of Rights. When the Court invalidates Congressional action because inconsistent with this understanding of the procedural restraints on the process of national lawmaking, the merits of the legislation in question are left open for reconsideration by Congress. It is the process of lawmaking, not the substance of the statute in question, that the Court reviews. These structural limits on the national legislative process can therefore be understood as providing related means to reinforce the ability of the people's elected representatives to legislate substantive ends.*

First, the Court can assure that the process of political change is open and genuinely representative so that all of the people can make their voices heard and no particular group once elected to Congress is ever free from accountability to the people. Similarly, the Court may choose to interpret the first amendment to assure that political debate is genuinely open rather than constrained by any person, party or point of view in power. Without such protection for the process of national election and political decision making, representative democracy does not even deserve the name. With such protection of these representation-reinforcing values, the people will be able to participate through their elected representatives. The people may continually respond to changed circumstances and evaluate the effectiveness, integrity, and propriety of existing policies and consider new alternatives. An independent judiciary *is* uniquely suited to deciding cases and controversies when the other branches of government seek to shortcut this constitutional process of representative democracy. This much is common ground with Ely's particular elaboration of judicial review.[66]

Second, the Court can assure that there are not other structural defects in the national lawmaking process resulting either from a failure by Congress to focus on the merits of the issues in legislating or from ongoing prejudice by a majority "in-group" seeking to impose or to perpetuate a position of subordinate caste on a minority "out-group." The first type of defect is particularly crucial in those cases in which Congress is

*In matters involving separation of powers between the three branches of the federal government, the Court also eschews review of the substance of the policy choices made by the other branches of government. The Court merely referees disputes between the executive and Congress and protects its own jurisdiction from unauthorized congressional regulation in a similar fashion. *See, e.g.,* Marbury v. Madison, 5 U.S. (1 Cranch) 137 (1803); Youngstown Sheet & Tube Co. v. Sawyer, 343 U.S. 579 (1952); United States v. Nixon 418 U.S. 683 (1974); Chadha v. I.N.S., 462 U.S. 819 (1986). As a result, the substantive values that should control in these cases also remain ultimately in the hands of the people through their elected officials. For example, when the Court ruled that President Truman could not unilaterally act to seize the steel mills in *Sawyer,* the merits of seizing steel mills remained open for consideration by Congress by ordinary legislation. When the Court ruled that neither the House nor the Senate acting alone could "veto" a federal agency rule or regulation in *Chadha,* Congress remained free to enact ordinary legislation pursuant to the procedure set forth in section 7 of Article I to overturn agency proceedings. And when Chief Justice Marshall held that Congress could not expand the *original* jurisdiction of the Supreme Court to issue a writ of mandamus against the Secretary of State in *Marbury,* Congress retained the power under Article III to empower lower federal courts to issue such orders against executive officials, with *appellate* review in the Supreme Court.

seeking to legislate a different result for the nation concerning what the Court has declared under provisional review are the privileges or immunities of United States citizens as against the states. If there is to be any kind of meaningful national dialogue over the content of such fundamental national rights, the people's representatives in Congress have an obligation to raise and to decide such issues frontally on the merits. Unless such clear statements of congressional intent to override the Court's judgment are made, Congress may inadvertently resolve the issue without even understanding itself what is being decided, let alone allowing the people to debate the issue publicly.[67] Ely is not concerned with this problem, no doubt because he does not see how the Court's initial declaration of substantive values can be made consistent with representative democracy.[68]

Guarding against the second type of defect is vital if the democracy is not to be tainted by systemic bias based on the majority's prejudice toward any minority group that the majority chooses to single out for disregard. Ely's particular elaboration of representation-reinforcing review seeks to determine whether legislation has been motivated, for example, by a white majority "in-group's" attempt to discriminate against a black minority "out-group." Ely's "we-they" approach fails to take account of the constitutional sources, importance, and difficulty of those aspects of provisional review that can protect against all caste-based defects in the congressional lawmaking process.[69] Chapter 3 therefore also elaborates a wider-ranging anticaste principle to guide this aspect of judicial review of the congressional lawmaking process.

Ultimately, however, provisional review leaves *most* of the substantive decisions on how resources should be allocated and how *most* of our fundamental values should be defined to the people through their representatives in Congress precisely because the Bill of Rights can be read as *not* protecting many substantive rights. In this national political process, the Court retains an essential role, first, in stimulating the dialogue over the meaning of the Constitution and second, in shaping the national political process to assure that it is open, fair, informed, and not skewed by systemic caste discrimination.

While the first part of the book develops the theory of provisional review from the text and structure of the Constitution and some of the Court's landmark rulings, it would be misleading to leave the impression that any Justice has ever adopted provisional review in any opinion, except in a relatively narrow range of federalism cases. For the broader range of human rights controversies under the Constitution, the Court still holds that its interpretation is final and that Congress generally lacks authority to legislate a different answer. The second part of the book therefore explores how provisional review could operate in personal rights cases if the theory were ever embraced by the Court. Part II uses hypothetical cases, opinions, and disagreements among mythical Justices because no prior judicial rulings exist from which to make any more traditional form of legal analysis. Chapter 4 deals with free speech, chapter 5 with discrimination, chapter 6 with abortion, and chapter 7 with education.

Provisional review springs from one reading of the federal structure of the Constitution. One of the Court's primary functions is to protect national interests from state abridgment in the first instance. Section 1 of the fourteenth amendment authorizes the Court to articulate a broad range of national rights that the States may not violate. Congress, under its plenary article I legislative power, may then enact a different national policy. To the full extent the Court determines that the Bill of Rights is narrower than section 1 of the fourteenth amendment, the Court itself will choose not to invalidate such congressional legislation as violating any substantive rights. Indeed, with a relatively few exceptions, the Court will examine only the *process* of lawmaking under the Bill of Rights (and separation of power doctrines). As a result, most judicial invalidations of congressional acts will merely remit the particular substantive policy choice of the statute back to Congress for *reconsideration* through a process that *is* open, fundamentally fair, and focused on the merits of the substantive policy at issue. Part II explores the surprising potential of provisional review to generate a meaningful dialogue between the Court and the people over the meaning of the Constitution.

Conclusion

Provisional review provides an alternative form of judicial review in which the Court may act on the basis of principle to stimulate and to oversee a national dialogue on substantive rights. The Court raises these issues for national decision when it posits (or refuses to posit) an individual right under the fourteenth amendment as supreme against a conflicting state policy choice. So long as the national lawmaking process does not run afoul of the restrictions of the Bill of Rights, Congress—acting through its enumerated powers—may then enact legislation ratifying, revising, or rejecting the substantive policy initially adopted by the Court. Provisional review therefore answers John Ely's question of how the Court can address substantive rights issues under open-ended constitutional provisions consistent with the nation's commitment to representative democracy. Indeed, for those conservatives or progressives who wish to allow the states to operate as diverse laboratories of democracy to experiment with different answers, Congress may respond to the Court's initial ruling declaring a national privilege or immunity under the fourteenth amendment simply by authorizing the states to adopt their own answers.

Provisional review also responds to Alexander Bickel's disenchantment with the Court providing the final answers to the elusive and ongoing search for fundamental values. It allows the Court to engage in a principled dialogue with the people over the right answers to moral questions. The Court can posit what it believes *should* be the national rights of the individual, without finally stifling the people's will or silencing the voice of the Court. It provides a framework for raising, answering, and revisiting questions that may have enduring appeal for liberals and conservatives, regardless of their hopes for or fears of particular Justices now sitting or those appointed to the Court in the future.

Finally, provisional review provides one answer to the dilemma of judicial choice under our Constitution. The text and structure of the Constitution and the framers' intent authorize the conscientious Justice to adopt such a provisional approach to judicial review that is consistent with our nation's (and the Constitution's) commitment to representative democracy in our federal system. A caution, however, is in order. Provisional review itself is *only* a choice: although it is authorized, it is not compelled by the text and structure of the Constitution.[70] Given the already proven ways in which the Court's supposedly final decisions have been reversed, modified, or eroded over time in the past, the question remains whether it is *wise* for the Court expressly to embrace this reading.

The fiction of the Supreme Court as the final arbiter in *all* constitutional cases has served to compel the people to give at least a respectful second look at the merits of legislation overturned by the Court. If the fiction were uncovered by the Court's explicit embrace of provisional review, it is possible that the Congress would feel free to run roughshod over the Court's point of view; and the people might then lose respect for the Court altogether. There are also real dangers if the Court were to recognize congressional power under article I to revise the Court's fourteenth amendment rulings but refused to embrace the extent and importance of the Court's role in shaping the national dialogue and protecting individual and minority interests in the national political process. It is conceivable that the Court would just rubber stamp the process of congressional lawmaking rather than grapple seriously with the issue of whether the legislation was tainted by caste discrimination or other structural defects.

Given the already proven ways by which the people have engaged in some dialogue with the Court over the meaning of the Constitution, it is therefore appropriate for the Court to proceed cautiously with provisional review by choosing at the outset to make substantive rights rulings as against the states binding only under the privileges or immunities rather than the due process clause of the fourteenth amendment. Whether the Court then adopts provisional review or moves over time within a more plainly flexible framework of final review is not as critical as assuring that the national dialogue on substantive rights is not stilled.

In the decades ahead, the greater risk is that national debate will be stifled, either by a liberal court claiming to be the final fount of all wisdom on substantive rights or a conservative court saying that the framers intended that the individual have almost no rights as against the states or that the Congress lacks authority as against the states to promote the national welfare or individual rights. Either swing would serve as an unwarranted judicial attempt to silence national political debate. Neither would serve the commands of the Constitution or the needs of our representative democracy.

Provisional review, therefore, will have served a useful purpose if it convinces the majority of the Justices, pundits on all sides of the political spectrum, and the people to be *skeptical* of claims that the Constitution provides a single, simple answer for every question and that Supreme Court rulings should be final because the Justices can divine how the framers specifically intended to resolve all of the constitutional cases that come before the Court. Whatever the merits of the details of provisional review elaborated in this book, the theory provides a new way of understanding how the Court's rulings posit *one* interpretation that begins rather than ends a dialogue with the people over the meaning of the Constitution. Once the Justices and the people candidly accept the burden of judicial choice thereby vested in the Court in interpreting the Constitution and applying its provisions to specific cases, the Court, the commentators, and the people can get on with the task of keeping our Constitution alive for generations to come by continuing the resulting national dialogue over the meaning of the Constitution. The framers may not have given specific answers to many of the important questions that confront the nation, but the Constitution does establish a representative democracy and federal system under which we the people have the opportunity to debate these issues openly and the responsibility to continue to decide them for ourselves.

NOTES

1. Wellington, *Revisiting* The People and the Court, 95 YALE L.J. 1565, 1567 (1986).
2. C. BLACK, THE PEOPLE AND THE COURT 52–53 (1960).
3. For example, in Plessy v. Ferguson, 163 U.S. 537 (1896), and Giles v. Harris, 189 U.S. 475 (1903), the Court held that the states had the power under the Constitution to impose racial segregation and to exclude blacks from voting. These decisions placed the Court's voice squarely behind the newly framed Jim Crow laws. Within a decade, the states enacted countless laws and approved even more customs that effectively shot a color line through American life and subjugated blacks to a subordinate caste for decades to come. *See* Dimond, *The Anti-Caste Principle*, 30 WAYNE L. REV. 1, 18–21 (1983); C. V. WOODWARD, THE STRANGE CAREER OF JIM CROW (1957). As another example, the Warren Court's broad support for congressional

laws passed to challenge the resulting color bar fueled the civil rights movement in the 1960s. *See* Katzenbach v. McClung, 379 U.S. 294 (1964); South Carolina v. Katzenbach, 383 U.S. 301 (1966); and Dimond, *supra,* 30 WAYNE L. REV. at 26–30. *Cf. also* Jones v. Mayer, 392 U.S. 409 (1968) (expansive interpretation of the 1866 Civil Rights Act).

4. *See, e.g.,* Garcia v. San Antonio Metropolitan Transit Auth., 469 U.S. 528, 557 (1985); U.S. v. Scott, 437 U.S. 82, 86–87 (1979); Edelman v. Jordan, 415 U.S. 651, 671 (1974), quoting Burnett v. Coronado Oil & Gas Co., 285 U.S. 393, 406–08 (1932) (Brandeis, J., dissenting).
5. Thus, for example, the Court's rulings in *Plessy* and *Giles* upholding the power of the states to impose racial caste (*see* note 3 *supra*) were not, ultimately, respected. Over the years, they were eventually distinguished, eroded, and finally overruled without the benefit of any constitutional amendment. In a series of cases the Court held that various forms and finally all state-mandated exclusion and segregation *do* violate the fourteenth and fifteenth amendments. *See* United States v. Guinn, 238 U.S. 347 (1915); Buchanan v. Warley, 245 U.S. 60 (1917); Lane v. Wilson, 307 U.S. 275 (1939); Shelley v. Kramer, 334 U.S. 1 (1948); McLaurin v. Oklahoma State Regents, 339 U.S. 637 (1950); Brown v. Bd. of Educ. 347 U.S. 483 (1954); Loving v. Virginia, 388 U.S. 1 (1967); and Dimond, *supra,* 30 WAYNE L. REV. at 21–30. If the Modern Court had blindly adhered to *stare decisis* in these cases, it is difficult to imagine how the dominant majorities in the states or Congress would have acted voluntarily to remedy Jim Crow segregation and exclusion without the encouragement of the Court, as well as the concerted protest of the outcast minority.
6. *See, e.g.,* Reagan, *Remarks* in THE GREAT DEBATE: OUR WRITTEN CONSTITUTION 53–56 (1986).
7. *See Nomination of Robert H. Bork to be Associate Justice of the United States Supreme Court: Hearings before Committee on Judiciary, United States Senate,* 100th Cong., 1st Sess. (1987).
8. *Id.*
9. *Id.*
10. The eventual confirmation of Anthony Kennedy, however, demonstrated the limits of the process of Senate review of the judicial views of most Supreme Court nominees. When President Reagan dropped the ideological battle over the role of the Supreme Court, and when his nominee's record and responses were relatively low in profile, content, and controversy, the Senate acquiesced in the President's choice without having much idea how the new Justice might choose to decide hard cases in the future.
11. *E.g.,* J. ELY, DEMOCRACY AND DISTRUST 1–2 (1980). *See also* M. PERRY, THE CONSTITUTION, THE COURTS, AND HUMAN RIGHTS 10–11 (1980); Bork, *The Constitution, Original Intent, and Economic Rights,* 23 SAN DIEGO LAW REV. 823, 824–26 (1986); Dimond, *Provisional Review,* 12 HASTINGS CONST. L.Q. 201, 203 (1985); Grano, *Judicial Review and a Written Constitution,* 28 WAYNE L. REV. 1–8 (1981).
12. Marbury v. Madison, 5 U.S. (1 Cranch) 137 (1803).
13. Of course, it is instructive that

Chief Justice Marshall's interpretations of the meaning of section 3 of Article III and of the Court's power of judicial review were *not* compelled by text of the Constitution or by the intent of the framers. *See, e.g.,* L. TRIBE, AMERICAN CONSTITUTIONAL LAW 25 (1988). Marshall simply "resolved the indeterminancy [of the constitutional text and framing], in essence, by *postulating* that federal courts have the power" of judicial review. *Id.* (emphasis in original).

14. *See, e.g.,* R. BERGER, GOVERNMENT BY JUDICIARY 2–3, 362–72, 407–08 (1977); Grano, *supra* note 11.
15. *E.g.,* A. BICKEL, THE LEAST DANGEROUS BRANCH 102–05 (1962); Dimond, *Strict Construction and Judicial Review of Racial Discrimination under the Equal Protection Clause,* 80 MICH. L. REV. 462, 494–502, 506–07 (1982). *See, generally,* H. FLACK, THE ADOPTION OF THE FOURTEENTH AMENDMENT (1908); and THE FEDERALIST PAPERS.
16. J. ELY, *supra* note 11, at 2; Sandalow, *Constitutional Interpretation,* 79 MICH. L. REV. 1033, 1036, 1039, 1064–68 (1981).
17. *E.g.,* Rochin v. California, 342 U.S. 165 (1950); Griswold v. Connecticut, 381 U.S. 479 (1965); Stanley v. Georgia, 394 U.S. 557 (1969); Boddie v. Connecticut, 401 U.S. 371 (1971); Roe v. Wade, 410 U.S. 113 (1973); and Moore v. East Cleveland, 431 U.S. 494 (1977). Pierce v. Society of Sisters, 268 U.S. 510 (1925), and Meyer v. Nebraska, 262 U.S. 390 (1923), were precursors to this doctrinal line of development.
18. *See, e.g.,* Remarks of Attorney General Meese, quoted in ABA JOURNAL, Feb. 1, 1987, at 66–67. *See also* R. BERGER, *supra* note 14, at 249–82, 300–05; Grano *supra* note 11. The irony is that conservative Justices who cherished judicial restraint, like Harlan, embraced the substantive due process inquiry that today's conservatives decry. *See Griswold v. Connecticut, supra.*
19. Dred Scott v. Sandford, 60 U.S. (19 How.) 393 (1857).
20. *E.g.,* Lochner v. New York, 198 U.S. 45 (1905). *See, generally,* W. LOCKHART, Y. KAMISAR & J. CHOPER, CONSTITUTIONAL LAW 433–39 (1980).
21. Lochner v. New York, 198 U.S. at 75 (Holmes, J., dissenting).
22. *See, e.g.,* West Coast Hotel v. Parrish, 300 U.S. 379 (1937); NLRB v. Jones & Laughlin Steel Co., 301 U.S. 1 (1937); Lincoln Federal Labor Union v. Northwestern Iron & Metal Co., 348 U.S. 483 (1955); Ferguson v. Skrupa, 372 U.S. 726 (1963).
23. *See, e.g.,* Fiss & Krauthammer, *The Rehnquist Court,* NEW REPUBLIC, March 10, 1982, at 14; Meese, *Speech, reprinted in* THE GREAT DEBATE: INTERPRETING OUR WRITTEN CONSTITUTION 8–9 (1986); Meese Remarks, *supra* note 18; Schmidt, *The Rehnquist Court: A Watershed,* NEW YORK TIMES 27 (June 22, 1986); *The Bork Nomination,* NEW YORK TIMES 12 (July 9, 1987); *Notes and Comment,* THE NEW YORKER 17 (Aug. 3, 1987); Dworkin, *The Bork Nomination,* NEW YORK REVIEW OF BOOKS 3 (Aug. 13, 1987); and note 6.
24. *Cf., e.g.,* Meese, *Speech, supra* note 23, at 8–9; Epstein, *Needed: Activist Judges for Economic Rights,* WALL STREET JOURNAL 32 (Nov. 14, 1985); R. BERGER, *supra* note 14; H. MEYER, THE HISTORY AND

MEANING OF THE FOURTEENTH AMENDMENT (1977); B. SIEGAN, ECONOMIC LIBERTIES AND THE CONSTITUTION (1980).

25. *See, e.g.*, A. BICKEL, *supra* note 15, at 102–05; J. ELY, *supra* note 11, at 28, 38, 41; C. FAIRMAN, RECONSTRUCTION AND REUNION, Part 1, 1297, 1387–88 (1971); Bork, *Neutral Principles and Some First Amendment Problems*, 47 IND. L.J. 1, 13–15, 17–19 (1971); Grano, *supra* note 11, at 61–75; Sandalow, *supra* note 16, at 1036, 1045–46, 1054–55, 1061–62, 1067–68, 1072; VanAlstyne, *A Graphic Review of the Free Speech Clause*, 70 CAL. L. REV. 107, 148–50 (1982). *But see* R. BERGER, *supra* note 14.
26. *See, e.g.*, Bickel, *The Original Understanding and the Segregation Decision*, 69 HARV. L. REV. 1 (1955); A. BICKEL, *supra* note 15, at 59–63, 102–05; J. ELY, *supra* note 11, at 22–30; Dimond, *supra* note 15. *But see* R. BERGER, *supra* note 14.
27. Judge Bork, an avowed interpretivist, recently noted that "the Bill of Rights and the Civil War amendments . . . have limits. . . . [For example,] freedom from unreasonable searches and seizures does not protect the power of businesses to set prices. These limits mean that the judge's authority has limits and *outside* the designated areas democratic institutions govern." *The Constitution, Original Intent, and Economic Rights*, 23 SAN DIEGO L. REV. 823, 825 (1986) (emphasis supplied). This does *not*, however, resolve the dilemma of judicial choice: *within* the range of alternative choices authorized by the Constitution (e.g., the meaning of free speech, equal protection, and privileges or immunities), the judge is *not* given an answer but must make a choice. Review of the historical materials surrounding the framing of a particular clause may provide some additional limits. But, as Judge Bork earlier recognized (*see, Neutral Principles and Some First Amendment Problems*, 47 IND. L.J. 1, 13–15, 17–19 (1971)), it will rarely eliminate the burden of judicial choice in deciding the meaning of general phrases by eliminating all but one alternative reading. *See also* Monaghan, *Stare Decisis and Constitutional Adjudication*, 88 COL. L. REV. 723, 772 (1988).
28. 163 U.S. 537 (1896).
29. 347 U.S. 483 (1954).
30. One response to this dilemma of judicial choice is to choose not to choose: unless the framers clearly and specifically agreed to outlaw the particular practice (e.g., segregation) in question, a Justice could just throw up her hands and hold that there is no constitutional limit on legislative discretion. But this choice may also fail to implement the intent of the framers and the meaning of the constitutional text. General phrases, not specifically restricted by the framers, authorize future Courts to make a reasoned decision on how to articulate and to apply the general principle to decide the specific case or controversy at hand. The choice not to choose does not resolve the dilemma of judicial choice. At best, it only seeks to have the judiciary abdicate its responsibility to interpret the meaning of much of the Constitution in deciding cases within its jurisdiction; but this may also serve to place the full weight of the Court's authority and

prestige behind the policy choice enacted by the legislature. *See* note 3 *supra*.

31. *See* sources in note 26 *supra*; and Grano, *supra* note 11, at 67–73.
32. A. BICKEL, *supra* note 15; Bickel, *supra* note 26.
33. *See* A. BICKEL, *supra* note 15.
34. Bickel, *The Passive Virtues*, 75 HARV. L. REV. 40 (1961).
35. A. BICKEL, THE SUPREME COURT AND THE IDEA OF PROGRESS (1970); A. BICKEL, THE MORALITY OF CONSENT (1975).
36. Michael Perry, a more active defender of the Supreme Court's judicial activism, recently has trumpeted the judiciary's role in engaging in a reasoned search for right answers to such fundamental moral questions. THE CONSTITUTION, THE COURTS, AND HUMAN RIGHTS (1980). Given the Court's relative independence from majoritarian pressures of the moment, it *is* in a uniquely functional position to address such issues and lead the country by promoting a dialogue over fundamental values. The Court can act, as Eugene Rostow observed, as an "educational body, and the Justices are inevitably teachers in a vital national seminar." *The Democratic Character of Judicial Review*, 66 HARV. L. REV. 193, 208 (1963). Recognizing the antimajoritarian nature of unelected oracles finally imposing their own answers to such moral questions on the people, however, Perry does provide for one majoritarian failsafe: if the people don't like the answer provided by the Court on any issue, Congress may simply remove the Court's jurisdiction to opine on cases raising that particular question. For one who proclaims the functional need for reasoned moral dialogue by the Court, however, such a purportedly democratic solution would serve only to silence the voice of the Court altogether.
37. J. ELY, *supra* note 11, at 71–72.
38. *Id.*; Ely *The Wages of Crying Wolf: A Comment on Roe v. Wade*, 82 YALE L.J. 920 (1973).
39. J. ELY, *supra* note 11, at 22–30.
40. J. ELY, *supra* note 11, at 41.
41. J. ELY, *supra* note 11, at 18–21, 95–98.
42. J. ELY, *supra* note 11, at 102–79.
43. J. ELY, *supra* note 11, at 181.
44. J. ELY, *supra* note 11, at 41.
45. Sandalow, *Judicial Protection of Minorities*, 75 MICH. L. REV. 1162, 1187–90 (1977); Wellington, *Book Review*, 97 HARV. L. REV. 326, 335 (1983); Wellington, *The Nature of Judicial Review*, 91 YALE L.J. 486, 504–20 (1982). *Cf.* G. CALABRESI, A COMMON LAW FOR THE AGE OF STATUTES (1982).
46. *See, e.g.*, U.S. CONST amend. XI (overriding Chisholm v. Georgia, 2 U.S. (2 Dall.) 419 (1793)); U.S. CONST. amend. XIV, sec. 1 (overriding Dred Scott v. Sandford, 60 U.S. (19 How.) 393 (1857)); U.S. CONST. amend. XVI (overriding Pollock v. Farmers' Loan & Trust Co., 157 U.S. 429 (1895)); U.S. CONST. amend. XXVI (overriding Oregon V. Mitchell, 400 U.S. 112 (1970)).
47. *Compare, e.g.*, Brown v. Bd. of Educ., 347 U.S. 483 (1954) *with* Plessy v. Ferguson, 163 U.S. 537 (1896); NLRB v. Jones & Laughlin Steel Corp., 301 U.S. 1 (1937) and United States v. Darby, 312 U.S. 100 (1941) *with* Hammer v. Dagenhart, 247 U.S. 251 (1918); West Coast Hotel v. Parrish, 300 U.S. 379 (1937) and Lincoln Federal Labor Union v. Northwestern Iron and Metal Co., 335 U.S. 525 (1949) *with* Lochner v.

New York, 198 U.S. 45 (1905); and Garcia v. San Antonio Metropolitan Transit Auth., 469 U.S. 528 (1985) *with* National League of Cities v. Usery, 426 U.S. 833 (1976).

48. *See, e.g.*, NLRB v. Virginia Elec. & Power Co., 314 U.S. 469 (1941); Kent v. Dulles, 357 U.S. 116 (1958); Swann V. Charlotte-Mecklenberg Board of Education, 402 U.S. 1, 16–18 (1971); Quern v. Jordan, 440 U.S. 332, 340–45 (1979); and Penhurst State School v. Halderman, 451 U.S. 1, 15–17 and n. 13 (1981).

49. For example, the *Lochner* Court's review of the "reasonableness" of federal and state economic and welfare regulation did not end with a constitutional amendment, new appointments to the Court, or even an explicit rejection of doctrine. Instead, it ended as the Court finally responded to the continuing wave of legislation in the New Deal by approving statutes under the "reasonableness" test that it would have previously ruled unconstitutional under *Lochner*. Thereafter, the Modern Court's doctrine evolved into a "rational basis test" that explicitly overruled *Lochner* in keeping with more deferential review of such social welfare legislation. *See* text at notes 20–22 *supra*. Recently, the same type of evolutionary process led, first, to the limitation and, finally, to the overruling of Justice Rehnquist's similar attempt to evaluate the necessity of federal legislation passed pursuant to Congress's plenary power under the commerce clause that impacted the sovereignty of the states. *See* chapter 2, *infra* at note 17.

50. Wellington, Book Review, 97 HARV. L. REV. 326, 335 (1983).

51. J. ELY, *supra* note 11, at 187 n. 13.

52. J. CHOPER, JUDICIAL REVIEW AND THE NATIONAL POLITICAL PROCESS, 205–09 (1980). *See also* C. BLACK, STRUCTURE AND RELATIONSHIP IN CONSTITUTIONAL LAW 13–17, 19–20 (1969); Dowling, *Interstate Commerce and State Power,* 27 VA. L. REV. 1 (1940); Monaghan, *Constitutional Common Law,* 89 HARV. L. REV. 1, 13–17 (1975); Sedler, *The Negative Commerce Clause as a Restriction on State Regulation,* 31 WAYNE L. REV. 885 (1985); Wechsler, *The Political Safeguards of Federalism,* 54 COL. L. REV. 543 (1954).

53. J. CHOPER, *supra* note 52, at 60–170.

54. *See, e.g.*, Heart of Atlanta Motel, Inc. v. United States, 379 U.S. 241 (1964); and Katzenbach v. McClung, 379 U.S. 294 (1964). *Cf.* Fitzpatrick v. Bitzer, 427 U.S. 445 (1976).

55. The recent controversy over Congress's power under section 5 of the fourteenth amendment to enforce section 1 by overriding the Court's interpretation of rights protected under section 1 is thereby avoided. *See* chapter 3 *infra*. It is enough to note here that section 5 of the fourteenth amendment provides at most *another* source of power to do what Congress already has the power to do under section 8 of article I.

56. McCulloch v. Maryland, 17 U.S. 316, 430–33 (1819); Gibbons v. Ogden, 22 U.S. 1 (1824); and Martin v. Hunter's Lessee, 14 U.S. 304 (1816).

57. McCulloch v. Maryland, 17 U.S. at 406.

58. McCulloch v. Maryland, 17 U.S. at 431.

59. *See, e.g.*, United States v. Darby,

312 U.S. 100 (1941) overruling Hammer v. Dagenhart, 247 U.S. 251 (1918); Garcia v. San Antonio Metropolitan Transit Auth., 469 U.S. 528 (1985) overruling National League of Cities v. Usery, 426 U.S. 833 (1976); Fitzpatrick v. Bitzer, 427 U.S. 445 (1976); J. Choper, *supra* note 52, at 176–92; Dimond, *supra* note 11, at 210–15; and Wechsler, *supra* note 52, at 547–52.

60. Cooper v. Aaron, 358 U.S. 1 (1958).
61. Former Attorney General Meese apparently disagrees with this understanding of the state's duty to respect the Supreme Court's rulings. *Remarks* quoted in ABA Journal 66–67 (Feb. 1, 1987). It is true in the *Cooper* case that Governor Faubus was not personally bound by the judgment in *Brown* in the sense of being subject to contempt for violating the terms of the Court's decree in *Brown*; neither the Governor nor his predecessors in interest were parties to *Brown*. As a state official, however, Governor Faubus had a duty under section 1 of the fourteenth amendment and the supremacy clause not to deny equal protection of the laws to any person, including, for example, by promoting segregation of Little Rock public school children in violation of the Supreme Court's interpretation of the meaning of the fourteenth amendment in *Brown*.
62. Mitchum v. Foster, 407 U.S. 225, 242 (1975).
63. To implement this reading, the Court would have to create a new line of development for the privileges or immunities clause, which has been stunted since the 1873 ruling in the Slaughter-House Cases, 83 U.S. 76 (1873), that an individual's interest in engaging in a particular trade or business is not such a national right. While this particular result is unexceptional, Court rulings thereafter chose to review just such substantive value choices under the due process clause. *See, e.g.*, text at notes 17 and 20–22 *supra*. The Court, under provisional review, would choose instead to make reasoned choices about what substantive rights represent national privileges or immunities that the states may not infringe, no matter how fair the process.
64. Marbury v. Madison, 5 U.S. (1 Cranch) 137 (1803).
65. *See, generally*, Heart of Atlanta Motel, Inc. v. United States, 379 U.S. 241, 254–58 (1964); Katzenbach v. McClung, 379 U.S. 294, 303–04 (1964); L. Tribe, American Constitutional Law 350 and n. 98 (1988); Cohen, *Congressional Power to Interpret Due Process and Equal Protection*, 27 Stan L. Rev. 603 (1975). (Although professors Cohen and Tribe agree with this understanding of the constitutional structure, they argue that the due process clause of the fifth amendment imposes the same restrictions on Congress as section 1 of the fourteenth amendment imposes on the states, including with respect to substantive rights. Under provisional review the fifth amendment due process clause would generally be interpreted as limited to fair process. *See* Dimond, *supra* note 11, at 223–20. The practical differences between the two interpretations will be explored in chapters 3–7).
66. *See* J. Ely, *supra* note 11, at 73–179.
67. There are a variety of additional ways in which the Court may re-

mit issues to Congress for another look. In cases involving statutory construction and executive or administrative action, for example, the Court may raise issues of constitutional concern without declaring prior acts of Congress unconstitutional.

68. J. Ely, *supra* note 11, at 125–31. Indeed, on such fundamental issues, Dean Ely might see that a "visible legislative process" is as critical to making the democratic process work as preventing Congress from delegating decisions on policy to unelected bureaucrats. *Compare* J. Ely, *supra* note 11, at 125–31 *with id.*, at 131–36.

69. *Compare* J. Ely, *supra* note 11, at 32–33, 135–79 *with* Dimond, *The Anti-Caste Principle*, 30 Wayne L. Rev. 1 (1983); Dimond, *supra* note 11, at 218–21, 224–26, and n. 101, 235–38; Dimond & Sperling, *Of Cultural Determinism and the Limits of Law*, 83 Mich L. Rev. 1065, 1080–87 (1986); and L. Tribe, American Constitutional Law 1515–21 (1988).

70. In this sense, provisional review represents an interpretivist approach, properly understood, to discerning the meaning of the Constitution. It shares the "insistence that the work of the political branches is to be invalidated only in accord with an inference whose starting point, whose underlying premise, is fairly discoverable in the Constitution." J. Ely, Democracy and Distrust 1–2 (1980), quoted approvingly in Bork, *The Constitution, Original Intent, and Economic Rights*, 23 San Diego L. Rev. 823, 826 (1986). The text, structure, and history of the Constitution all authorize provisional review as one legitimate approach to understanding the complexity of judicial review and reconciling the subtlety of judicial choice with representative democracy.

Part I

Provisional Review in Theory: Exploring the Indeterminate Nature and the Federal Structure of the Constitution

CHAPTER 1

Equal Protection and the Segregation Decisions: No Escaping the Burden of Judicial Choice

Section 1 of the fourteenth amendment provides in pertinent part, "No State shall . . . deny to any person within its jurisdiction the equal protection of the laws." The precise meaning of this general phrasing for every issue is not apparent from the text. The fourteenth amendment is, therefore, a prime example of the indeterminate nature of the Constitution: it does not tell even the most conscientious judge how to decide the specific case or controversy that comes before a court for decision.

Consider, for example, state-mandated segregation of the races. Does a state law that compels or authorizes the segregation of blacks and whites in separate facilities that are equal in all material respects "deny . . . the equal protection of the laws?" Does the answer differ depending on the type of facility, say common carriers versus schools or municipal parks versus jury boxes? Does it matter if the state legislature passed the segregation law with the purpose of oppressing one race in contrast to promoting public order and safety? Does the answer depend on what specific state actions the framers of the fourteenth amendment intended to prohibit even though the text speaks in general terms? What answer should the Court give if neither the text nor the history of the framing of the amendment disclose the specific meaning of the equal protection clause? What if some of the framers thought that the equal protection clause did not apply to certain practices when the general text was ratified as drafted without any express exceptions? What if the framers of the fourteenth amendment supported the equal protection clause by speaking at the same level of generality as the text itself and refused to address the issue of the clause's specific application in order to avoid controversy that might hinder ratification of the proposed amendment?

The United States Supreme Court confronted the meaning of the equal protection clause in two landmark segregation rulings. In 1896 in *Plessy v. Ferguson*,[1] the Court ruled that a Louisiana statute compelling railroad companies to provide "equal but separate accommodations for the white and colored races" did not deny equal protection of the laws. In *Brown v. Board of Education*[2] some fifty-eight years later, the Court overruled *Plessy* and held that state laws requiring the segregation of children in "separate but equal" elementary and secondary schools denied equal protection of the laws. Before analyzing whether the fourteenth amendment itself compelled or authorized either of these divergent choices, it may be instructive to compare how the *Plessy* and *Brown* Courts attempted to ascertain the meaning of the equal protection clause.

The Court's Segregation Rulings

In *Plessy* Justice Brown never once cited the legislative history of the framing and ratification of the fourteenth amendment in writing the opinion for the Court. Instead, he discussed prior Supreme Court rulings that wrestled with the meaning of the fourteenth amendment, state court rulings both before and after the passage of the fourteenth amendment, and customs and practices in some of the states and the District of Columbia before and after the adoption of the fourteenth amendment. Justice Brown conceded that the "object of the amendment was undoubtedly to enforce the absolute equality of the two races before law, but," he added, "in the *nature of things* it could not have been intended to abolish distinctions based on color, or to enforce social, as distinguished from political, equality, or a commingling of the two races upon terms unsatisfactory to either. Laws permitting, and even requiring, their separation in places where they are liable to be brought into contact do not necessarily *imply* the *inferiority* of either race to the other. . . ."[3]

In support of this limitation with respect to segregation of his otherwise apparently general understanding of the "object" of the fourteenth amendment, Justice Brown first cited the Massachusetts Supreme Court's 1850 ruling in *Roberts v. Boston* upholding separate but equal schooling for black and white schoolchildren.[4] For three reasons, this reliance on the *Roberts* ruling is curious: the Massachusetts court upheld school segregation only against attack under a *state* constitutional guarantee of equality; the Massachusetts ruling preceded the adoption of the fourteenth amendment by some fourteen years; and the Massachusetts legislature responded to the *Roberts* ruling by outlawing school segregation in 1855.[5] In any event, such rulings by some state courts and practices in some states before or after the adoption of the fourteenth amendment hardly serve to define the meaning of a constitutional amendment that even Justice Brown conceded had something to do with providing at least some measure of racial equality to blacks under law.

Justice Brown then proceeded to distinguish state-imposed segregation from the Supreme Court's previous interpretation of the fourteenth amendment in *Strauder v. West Virginia* and related cases.[6] In these cases, Justice Brown conceded, the Court had ruled that barring blacks from juries violated the equal protection clause because such racial exclusion "*implied* a legal *inferiority* in civil society, which lessened the security of the right of the colored race, and was a step towards reducing them to a condition of servility."[7] To the plaintiff's claim that the Louisiana segregation statute's "enforced separation of the two races stamps the colored race with [just such] a badge of inferiority,"[8] Justice Brown responded, "If this be so, it is not by reason of anything found in the act, but solely because the colored race chooses to put that construction upon it."[9]

This callous conclusion prompted Justice Harlan to dissent: "The arbitrary separation of citizens, on the basis of race, while they are on a public highway, is a badge of servitude wholly inconsistent with . . . the equality before the law established by the [fourteenth amendment]. . . . [The Louisiana segregation statute], practically, puts the brand of servitude and degradation upon a large class of fellow citizens, our equals before the law. The thin disguise of 'equal' accommodations for passengers in railroad coaches will not mislead anyone, or atone for the wrong this day done."[10] For Justice Harlan, "the real meaning" of Louisiana's segregation law was the plain fact that it proceeded "on the ground that colored citizens are so inferior and degraded that they cannot be allowed to sit in public coaches occupied by white citizens."[11] The Louisiana segregation statute was therefore in direct violation of Harlan's understanding of the primary purpose of section 1 of the fourteenth amendment, to assure that "there is in this country . . . no caste here."

In effect, Justice Brown's opinion concluded that Louisiana's statute requiring separate but equal railway coaches did not violate the equal protection clause because the Court found that it did not impose or otherwise imply the inferiority of blacks as a group compared to the white majority.[12] Justice Harlan dissented because he found that the very purpose of such segregation laws was to relegate blacks to just such a subordinate caste.

Whatever else may be said of Justice Brown's opinion for the Court, he did not even claim to find anything in the text or in the history of the framing of the fourteenth amendment that compelled a conclusion that the equal protection clause either permitted or prohibited state segregation statutes. In *Plessy* the Court, itself, *chose* to interpret the fourteenth amendment as permitting Louisiana to impose segregation in railway cars by statute. In his dissent, Justice Harlan predicted that the Court's choice would, "in time, prove to be quite as pernicious as the decision made by [the Supreme Court] in the *Dred Scott* case."[13] Whether Justice Brown's racially insulting rhetoric further fueled the fires of racial hostility, the Court's choice to place its imprimatur upon state segregation laws did give rise over the next decade to passage of hundreds of Jim Crow laws in many of the states and to implementation of Jim Crow practices throughout the country. What had been an open question as to how the dilemma of racial inequality in the United States would be played out after Reconstruction was closed by *Plessy*: the Court's choice put the force of law behind what would soon become the rule of Jim Crow.[14] The color line came to divide the entire nation as segregation became the American way of life.[15]

In *Brown* Chief Justice Warren wrote for a unanimous court in striking down state laws mandating segregation of the public schools as denying equal protection of the laws. Prior to rendering its ruling, the Court required a second briefing "largely devoted to the circumstances surrounding the adoption of the fourteenth amendment."[16] Pointedly, the questions posed by the Court asked the parties before the Court and the Attorney General of the United States to discuss, first, whether the framers of the fourteenth amendment intended that the amendment would abolish segregation in public schools; second, even if the framers did not intend that the amendment require the immediate abolition of public school segregation, whether the framers understood that either Congress under its section 5 legislative power or the Court under its judicial power could construe the amendment in light of future conditions to abolish such segregation; and, third, if the first two inquiries provided no clear answer, whether the Court in its judicial power could now construe the amendment to abolish segregation in public schools.[17] The parties and the Attorney General submitted extensive briefs on these questions, and the Court held a second oral argument devoted to these issues.[18]

After reviewing these materials and examining the historical record independently,[19] the Chief Justice concluded for the Court, "Although these sources cast some light, it is not enough to resolve the problem with which we are faced. At best, they are inconclusive."[20] The Chief Justice noted that proponents and opponents of the amendment might have had quite different hopes for and fears of its meaning and the extent of its application. He also noted "an additional reason for the inconclusive nature of the Amendment's history with respect to segregated schools." Free common schools had not even begun to take hold in the South, and public schooling in the North was still at a very rudimentary stage of development at the time the amendment was proposed in 1866 and ratified in 1868. "As a consequence," the Chief Justice continued, "it is not surprising that there should be so little in the history of the fourteenth amendment related to its intended effect on public education."[21] The framers did not provide the answer to the question of the constitutionality of public school segregation for the Warren Court. The Court in *Brown* would make its own choice of the meaning of the equal protection clause.

The opinion then canvassed prior Supreme Court interpretations of the amendment: "In the first cases in this Court construing the fourteenth amendment, decided shortly after its adoption, the Court interpreted it as proscribing all state-imposed discriminations against the Negro race."[22] From this perspective, the "doctrine of 'separate but equal' did not make its appearance in this Court until 1896 in the case of Plessy v. Ferguson, involving not education but transportation."[23] In evaluating the Court's rulings after *Plessy*, the Chief Justice noted that none addressed the validity of the separate but equal doctrine in the field of public education. For example, in each of the cases involving exclusion of individual black plaintiffs from state graduate schools previously reserved for whites only, "inequality was found in that specific benefits enjoyed by white students were denied to Negro students of the same educational qualifications."[24] As a result, the Court did not have to reexamine the separate but equal doctrine in order to grant relief requiring the whites-only graduate schools to admit the individual black plaintiffs. Nevertheless, in *Sweatt v. Painter*, "the Court expressly reserved decision on the question whether Plessy v. Ferguson should be held inapplicable to public education."[25]

In the four cases consolidated for appeal in *Brown* involving segregation of the public schools in Kansas, Delaware, Virginia, and South Carolina, Chief Justice Warren chose to confront the separate but equal doctrine directly. Rather than find material inequalities, the Court chose to address the cases as if the black and white schools were "equalized" with respect to all "tangible factors."[26] This permitted the Warren Court to focus on whether the "intangible" impact of segregation on the schoolchildren denied them equal protection of the laws in view of the flowering and importance of public education in 1954. "In approaching this problem," the Chief Justice chose not "to turn the clock back to 1868 when the amendment was adopted, or even to 1896 when Plessy v. Ferguson was written."[27] The Chief Justice found that state-mandated isolation of black children in separate grade schools and high schools "solely because of their race generates a feeling of inferiority as to their status in the community that may affect their hearts and minds in a way unlikely ever to be undone."[28]

Quoting the trial court's finding in the Kansas case that "the policy of separating the races is usually interpreted as denoting the inferiority of the Negro group," the Court held "any language in Plessy v. Ferguson contrary to this finding is rejected."[29] With that understatement, the Warren Court in *Brown* chose to overrule the *Plessy* Court's incredible rationale that Jim Crow laws had neither the purpose nor the effect of imposing a badge of inferiority on blacks as a group compared to the white majority.*

*Although the opinion in *Brown* by its own terms limited this holding to the "field of public education," the Warren Court thereafter summarily overturned without comment any remaining vestiges of the separate but equal doctrine in a series of per curiam decisions striking down state-mandated segregation in all variety of public facilities. Similarly, in the companion case to *Brown* involving segregation of the District of Columbia public schools, the Court held, "Segregation in public education is not reasonably related to any proper governmental objective, and thus it imposes on Negro children of the District of Columbia a burden that constitutes an arbitrary deprivation of their liberty in violation of the due process clause [of the

In its remedial ruling issued after another rebriefing and reargument, the Warren Court reiterated that more than just the rights of the individual black plaintiffs to transfer to previously all-white schools was at stake. In *Brown II* the Court permitted delay in the admission of the individual named plaintiffs to the whites-only schools because of the inevitable delays required to dismantle the entire *system* of dual schooling and to permit an orderly transition to a unitary *system* of public schooling.[30] Although the requirement that the states proceed with "all deliberate speed" to accomplish this goal would be frustrated for years to come, the Warren Court did make clear that segregation would no longer have the force of law behind it. Whatever else may be said of the choice made in *Brown,* it placed the full weight of the Supreme Court and its interpretation of the equal protection clause behind those who sought to eradicate rather than to continue the color line in America.

The Warren Court's decision in *Brown* did, however, share much in common with the Court's ruling in *Plessy*. Neither Court found its answer to the meaning of the equal protection clause in the history of the framing of the fourteenth amendment. Both Courts made their own choice as to whether state-imposed segregation violated the text's command that "No state shall . . . deny to any person . . . the equal protection of the laws." In answering *this* question, both Courts asked whether segregation laws were premised on an official implication of the inferiority of blacks as a race or otherwise sought to subordinate blacks as a group to an inferior caste. With respect to the opposite choices made by the two Courts in answering this question, Justice Harlan was surely right in stating that "no one [should] be so wanting in candor as to assert" that the segregation laws had any other purpose or effect.[31] *If* the *Plessy* and *Brown* Courts correctly framed the issue for decision, there is *no* doubt which ruling was right in 1896, 1954, or now.

The Framing of the Fourteenth Amendment

The question remains whether the *Plessy* and *Brown* courts focused on the correct issue. We must therefore explore whether the text, framing, and legislative history of the fourteenth amendment compel a different approach to evaluating the constitutionality of official segregation under the equal protection clause. For example, one can imagine a historical record that would demonstrate to any conscientious judge that the fram-

---

fifth amendment]." Once *Brown* exposed the *Plessy* Court's lie that segregation was not grounded in the white majority's branding of the black minority as an inferior caste, the systemic racial inequality inherent in official segregation became manifest, whether imposed at municipal drinking fountains, statehouses, national parks, or the public schools.

ers intended the general phrasing of section 1 as only a shorthand code, either (*a*) to protect a narrow and defined set of rights which specifically excluded segregated facilities, rail coaches, and public schools from its coverage[32] *or* (*b*) to protect against all forms of racial discrimination against blacks, including specifically state-imposed segregation in railroad coaches and schools.[33] In either case, the Justices could then arguably claim that the framers of the fourteenth amendment had already made the decision on the meaning of the equal protection clause with respect to segregated coaches and schools.[34]

The framing of the fourteenth amendment, however, does not so easily relieve the Court of the burden of choosing for itself. To provide an understanding of the necessity of judicial choice, we will review the amendment's relevant text, the framing of this language, and the debates on the House and Senate floor. All support the conclusion that, with the exception of suffrage for blacks (which was subsequently guaranteed by the adoption of the fifteenth amendment), the equal protection clause is an open-textured guarantee against discrimination. In each case, the Court must choose for itself how to interpret this protection.

The Text

Section 1 of the fourteenth amendment provides:

> All persons born or naturalized in the United States, and subject to the jurisdiction thereof, are citizens of the United States and of the State wherein they reside. No State shall make or enforce any law which shall abridge the privileges or immunities of citizens of the United States; nor shall any State deprive any person of life, liberty or property without due process of law; nor deny to any person within its jurisdiction the equal protection of the laws.

The first sentence relating to citizenship expressly overrode the prior judgment in *Dred Scott* that black persons were not to be viewed as citizens of the United States under the Constitution.[35] The second sentence is divided into three separate clauses. From the syntax, there is no indication that any of the clauses is meant to modify or limit the other. The first, the privileges or immunities clause, provides for substantive national rights; it does not, however, provide any list of what rights constitute such national privileges or immunities.[36]

The second, the due process clause, reads as if to provide for procedural fairness before depriving anyone of "life, liberty or property."[37] In this context, the third clause, the equal protection clause, is not limited by its terms to a nondiscrimination guarantee with respect to the national privileges or immunities in the first clause or life, liberty, or property described in the second clause. By its terms, the equal protection clause applies to all laws; its scope is not restricted by the text to some narrower subset of laws relating to certain subjects.[38] In sum, the text and syntax of the three clauses provide for three separate types of guarantees; and the scope of the equal protection guarantee is not limited to the subjects of the first two clauses.*

Finally, the three clauses of section 1 all impose duties directly on the states. The common object of their three separate commands is the state: "No State shall. . . ." And each of these commands appears to be self-executing in the sense of telling each state not to violate any of the three types of rights protected. Section 5 of the fourteenth amendment then adds, "The Congress shall have power to enforce, by appropriate legislation, the provisions of this article." Nine amendments provide Congress with this power to "enforce" the other provisions of the amendment. There is no indication from their text, or their relationship to the substantive provisions of the amendments, that they are intended to limit any of the direct obligations or rights contained in the amendments. Given the Court's judicial power to review cases and controversies to determine whether the Constitution has been violated, the congressional enforcement power in section 5 may be read to supplement, but it does not supplant the obligations imposed directly on the states by section 1.

The text and structure of the fourteenth amendment, therefore, appear to impose on the Court the burden of choosing how to interpret the nondiscrimination guarantee of the equal protection clause with respect to virtually all acts undertaken by the states. The constitutionality of segregation laws generally, and segregation laws with respect to railroad coaches and public schools specifically, are not exempt from judicial review under the equal protection clause as written and adopted in the fourteenth amendment.

The Framing

Two aspects of the framing of the fourteenth amendment intertwine to confound any historical evaluation. The process by which Congress

*The text of section 2 of the fourteenth amendment, however, does seem to imply that black suffrage may be beyond the intended scope of the equal protection guarantee. Section 2 provides that the apportionment of the representatives in the House shall be reduced to the extent that the right to vote is abridged in the states. Thus, if a state denied the vote to blacks, then only the white population would be counted in determining the number of representatives in the House for that state. This suggests that the otherwise general scope of the equal protection clause was not intended to cover discrimination against blacks with respect to voting. Within two years after adoption of the fourteenth amendment, the fifteenth amendment filled this gap: "The right of citizens of the United States to vote shall not be denied or abridged by the United States or by any State on account of race, color, or previous condition of servitude."

passed the 1866 Civil Rights Act and Representative John Bingham's statements opposing that act while framing sections 1 and 5 of the fourteenth amendment are not free from ambiguity.

While Bingham sat with the special Joint Committee of Fifteen on Reconstruction hearing evidence and debating the terms of an overall plan to deal with the rebel states, Senator Trumbull's Judiciary Committee proposed a civil rights bill. This 1866 Civil Rights Act was a response to the Black Codes, which the legislatures of the rebel states enacted immediately after the Civil War. The Confederacy may have lost the war and representatives of the rebel states been excluded from the halls of Congress, but the Conservative Democrats who gained control of the Southern statehouses were intent on preserving their system of racial caste after the adoption of the thirteenth amendment in 1865 abolished slavery and involuntary servitude. Many of these codes expressly excluded blacks from voting, owning land, making contracts, securing access to the courts, working without a special license, traveling without a pass, or engaging in certain trades.[39]

Other provisions, however, made no reference to race; for example, many of the vagrancy and apprenticeship laws applied on the surface to blacks and whites alike.[40] The invidious quality of these laws lay in their failure to protect blacks from the customary discrimination that left them without jobs or land; the vagrancy laws were then selectively enforced against blacks only and harsh penalties imposed in state courts. At the same time, white attacks on black persons and their property were studiously ignored by the local authorities. Blacks were in danger of being relegated to a status of virtual peonage. The federal military commanders overseeing Reconstruction reported to Congress that these laws, in combination with the racial discrimination practiced by white employers and landowners, would "reduce the freedmen to a condition of servitude worse than that from which they have been emancipated—a condition which will be slavery in all but its name."[41]

As drafted, the 1866 Civil Rights Act relied on Congress's power in section 2 of the thirteenth amendment to enforce section 1's abolition of slavery. The first section of the bill sought to protect against the sorts of evils described above. In addition to declaring that all persons were to be citizens, it commanded that there should be "no discrimination in civil rights . . . on account of race, color or previous condition of servitude" and then listed a number of the specific types of rights to be protected from such racial discrimination.[42] For its enforcement, the civil rights bill relied only on criminal prosecutions in federal courts against violators acting "under color of law."*[43] In the debates on the floor of the Senate in Janu-

*At the same time Trumbull also proposed a sweeping expansion to the Freedmen's Bureau. This bill was not proposed under Congress's power to enforce the thirteenth amendment's abolition of slavery, but under Congress's War Power under Article I, section 8. In addition to expanding the affirmative relief efforts to uplift

ary 1866, conservative opponents complained that the bill as written could be interpreted to outlaw all forms of racial discrimination, including antimiscegenation laws, exclusion of blacks from juries and voting, and segregated schools; the proponents responded by arguing that the bill as written was *not* intended to be that sweeping.[44]

Meanwhile, Bingham was busy in the Joint Committee on Reconstruction and finally convinced the Committee to present a proposal for an amendment to the Constitution that would clearly give Congress independent power to pass such civil rights legislation.[45] It provided: "The Congress shall have the power . . . to secure to the citizens of each state all privileges and immunities of citizens in the several states (Art. 4, sec. 2); and to all persons in the several states equal protection in the rights of life, liberty, and property (5th Amend.)."

Bingham's citation to the privileges and immunities clause of article IV, section 2 and to the fifth amendment's due process clause was apparently consistent with Bingham's initial view that these provisions should bind the states as the Constitution already stood without any amendment. In the debate on this proposal on the House floor in February 1866, Bingham argued, "Every word of the proposed amendment is today in the Constitution, save the words conferring the express grant of power upon the Congress of the United States. . . . [It] has been the want of the Republic that there was not an express grant of power in the Constitution to enable the whole people of every State, by congressional enforcement, to enforce obedience to these requirements of the Constitution. . . . [T]he proposed amendment does not impose upon any State of the Union, or any Citizen of the Union, any obligation which is not now enjoined upon them."[46] It did not bother Bingham that he substituted "equal protection" for "due process"; and, although this apparent reading of the existing constitutional obligations had been the darling of some of the abolitionists before the Civil War, the Supreme Court had never read the Bill of Rights as binding on the States, nor the privileges and immunities clause of article IV as anything more than a comity provision.[47]

Under questioning from the floor, Bingham eventually conceded that "the citizens must rely upon the States for their protection [of the Bill of Rights] . . . under the Constitution as it now stands."[48] He nevertheless argued that his proposed amendment would only enable Congress to enforce the protections that state officials *ought* always, under their oath under Article VI "to support this Constitution," to have provided to *all* persons, including the loyal Republicans and disenfranchised blacks who were then being crushed under the boot of Conservative Democrats in the

the new freedmen from conditions of servitude, poverty, and ignorance, it sought to protect blacks in rebel areas during the period of insurrection from racial discrimination in the "civil rights or immunities belonging to white persons" enumerated in the 1866 Civil Rights Acts.

Southern States.[49] In contrast to the floor debate on Trumbull's Civil Rights bill, when Conservatives charged that Bingham's proposal would empower Congress to outlaw segregated schools in Pennsylvania, for example, neither Bingham nor his Republican allies responded by suggesting that the scope of the proposal was more limited than that.[50]

But Bingham could not answer a quite different fear of some of his Republican friends: if a Congress hostile to the broad antidiscrimination protections envisioned by Bingham were subsequently to gain control, then "mere legislation" could undo all that might be gained in the thirty-ninth Congress. Rather than "leave it to the caprice of Congress," Republican Representative Hotchkiss concluded, "I want [these protections] secured [directly] by a constitutional amendment. Then if [Representative Bingham] wishes to go further, and provide by laws of Congress for the enforcement of those rights, I will go with him."[51] Bingham joined in postponing consideration of the amendment until it could be reworked in accord with this understanding.

While the Joint Committee on Reconstruction was redrafting the proposed fourteenth amendment, Trumbull's Civil Rights Bill came up for consideration on the House floor in March of 1866. During this debate, Bingham opposed the Civil Rights Bill, even while expressing his support for the Freedmen's Bureau Bill which protected exactly the same rights as the Civil Rights Bill.[52] Bingham argued, first, that the thirteenth amendment did not give Congress the power to legislate generally on civil rights because this protection of citizens was the primary responsibility and prerogative of the states under the Constitution. Although Bingham again reiterated that the states *ought* to guarantee to all of their citizens the Bill of Rights, he argued that the Constitution as it stood neither imposed these duties on the states nor empowered Congress to legislate them directly against the states. This lack of congressional power was precisely what Bingham's proposed constitutional amendment had been designed to correct; without such an amendment ratified by the people in the states themselves, Congress did not have authority to enact the Civil Rights Bill. In contrast, the Freedmen's Bureau Bill, which was more narrowly targeted at the rebel states, could be enacted during the period of insurrection under Congress's war powers under article I, section 8.

Second, Bingham argued that the reliance in Trumbull's bill on criminal enforcement was unjust. It would impose criminal sanctions on the public officials in virtually every state who acted in good faith in enforcing long-standing laws and customs of discrimination. Bingham argued that a constitutional amendment should instead be sent out to the people "to remedy the State wrong" of racial discrimination.[53]

In construing the "no discrimination in civil rights" provision of Trumbull's bill, Bingham added that it could not be narrowly limited: "civil rights" included all "social" and "political" rights, such as black suffrage, the right to hold public office, and the right to testify in court. To minimize his objections to the bill, Bingham therefore proposed that at least the criminal sanctions and the "no discrimination in civil rights" clause be deleted. In response to his fellow Republicans' concern about the nature of his opposition to the "no discrimination" clause, Bingham specifically denied that he should be understood as approving most state discrimination: "I make no captious objection to any legislation in favor of the rights of all before law." He added that the terms of the proposed Civil Rights Bill "should be the law of every State, by the voluntary act of every State. The law in every State should be just; it should be no respecter of persons. It is otherwise now, and it has been otherwise for many years in many States of the Union. I should remedy that not by an arbitrary assumption of power [by Congress] but by amending the Constitution of the United States, expressly prohibiting the States from any such abuse of power in the future."[54]

Although Bingham's proposals were initially defeated, the bill eventually came to a vote with the "no discrimination" clause deleted, but the criminal sanctions intact. Bingham continued to refuse to support the bill even though it finally was enacted over President Johnson's veto.[55] Although Bingham's opposition to the 1866 Civil Rights Act is not free from ambiguity, it is hard to read his comments and actions as suggesting that he held a narrow view of the meaning of "civil rights" or of the duties the states *ought* to owe their citizens to provide "equal protection."

In the Joint Committee on Reconstruction, Senator Stewart proposed "universal amnesty" for the rebel states in exchange for "universal suffrage" for blacks. This apparently did not fit the political realities facing the Republicans. Representative Stevens responded with a proposed amendment in five sections, the first providing for "no racial discrimination in civil rights," the second for black suffrage after July 4, 1876, and the fifth for congressional power to enforce; once adopted, Stevens proposed that rebel States could be readmitted to Congress after they had conformed their laws to the new amendment. Bingham repeatedly proposed changes in section 1, including more general language and the addition of the privileges or immunities, due process, and equal protection clauses. Despite several votes by the Committee to reject this approach, Bingham prevailed: on April 30, 1866, the Committee finally agreed to submit his proposal to Congress.[56]

Black suffrage had been dropped, and section 2 limited the basis for representation in the House to the extent suffrage for blacks was denied by any state. The Joint Committee also proposed two companion bills. The first provided for readmission of a rebel state upon its ratification of the amendment and conforming its laws to the amendment, while the second would disqualify Confederate leaders from holding public office.

Bingham's proposed section 1 read, "No State shall make or enforce any law which shall abridge the privileges or immunities of citizens of the United States; nor shall any State deprive any person of life, liberty or property without due process of law; nor deny to any person within its jurisdiction the equal protection of the laws." Section 5 read, "The Congress shall have the power to enforce, by appropriate legislation, the provisions of this article." In the subsequent debate on the House floor in May of 1866, Bingham defended his proposal with sweeping rhetoric and grand generalities.[57] Bingham conceded only one limit on the otherwise general scope of section 1: section 2 "excludes the conclusion" that the amendment would cover suffrage for blacks.[58]

In response to conservative complaints throughout the debate that the equal protection clause covered every other type of discrimination under the sun, Bingham never countered with any more limiting interpretation, or of the privileges or immunities clause for that matter. Consistent with his repeated statements in the past of the broad antidiscrimination duties and privileges or immunities that the states ought to afford to all of their citizens, Bingham did not attempt to narrow the reach of section 1 in the floor debates, except with respect to the exclusion of black suffrage by reference to the proposed amendment's text itself in section 2. Whatever his differences of opinion with his Republican colleagues over the scope and meaning of the "no discrimination in civil rights" clause deleted from the 1866 Civil Rights Act, Bingham drafted the different and more general phrasing of section 1 of the fourteenth amendment. Unlike the 1866 Civil Rights Act, Bingham's proposed section 1 of the fourteenth amendment contained no delineation of specific rights; and, on the floor of the House of Representatives, Bingham offered no narrowing construction of the general phrasing of the text. He just spoke in generalities as grand, and open-ended, as the text itself.[59]

In sum, although the matter is not entirely free from dispute, the framing of section 1 of the fourteenth amendment suggests that the text should be read as generally as its phrasing. The breadth of section 1's framing contrasts sharply with the delineation of specific rights, deletion of the "no discrimination" clause, and narrowing construction given in the legislative debates to the 1866 Civil Rights Act during this same period. The framing of the fourteenth amendment supports the conclusion that the equal protection clause applies to all actions of the states, with the exception of the denial of the vote to blacks. The framing of the equal protection clause left the task of interpreting its meaning as applied to specific issues up to future generations. In interpreting the meaning of the duty not to deny equal protection of the laws imposed directly on the states by section 1, there is nothing in the amendment's framing that relieved the *Plessy* Court or the *Brown* Court from the burden of judicial choice in deciding whether state-mandated segregation of railroad coaches or public schools denies equal protection of the laws.

The Debates in Congress

The bulk of the seven days of congressional debate in May and June of 1866 on the fourteenth amendment focused on the terms of Reconstruction as part of the ongoing power struggle of the moderate Republicans to achieve control in the face of opposition from Democrats, President Johnson, and conservative Republicans on the one hand and of pressure from radical Republicans on the other. As a result, more attention was paid to the three sections disqualifying rebel leaders from public office, reducing the representation of states that denied the freedmen the vote, and renouncing the Confederate debt than to the rights declared in section 1 and congressional enforcement power authorized in section 5. With respect to section 1, the proponents spoke in as general terms as the text in order to avoid political controversy.[60]

Not surprisingly therefore, "declamation abounded where hard analysis was wanting" in the debates on the two enduring sections.[61] Many of the speakers stated that a primary purpose of section 1 was to "constitutionalize" the 1866 Civil Rights Act, both to remove doubts expressed about the authority of Congress to pass the act under the thirteenth amendment and to remove the ability of any future Congress to repeal the act by ordinary legislation.[62] Such statements, however, do not mean that this was the *only* purpose for section 1 of the fourteenth amendment.[63]

In addition, others spoke generally about the broad scope of the privileges or immunities clause.[64] For example, Senator Howard, the primary sponsor in the Senate, suggested that the clause would "compel the States at all times to respect" (1) all of the types of rights listed "under . . . general heads" in a single Supreme Court Justice's opinion interpreting the privileges and immunities comity provision of article IV while hearing a case in a lower court, (2) the first eight amendments to the Constitution commonly known as the Bill of Rights, and (3) all other such "great fundamental guarantees." Howard also noted that this "mass of privileges, immunities, and rights" could not be "fully defined in their entire extent and precise nature."[65] Such generality is consistent with the constitutional text of the privileges or immunities clause: in contrast to the Civil Rights Act, it provides for a general set of national rights belonging to all citizens rather than a specific list of rights with respect to which blacks should be given the same treatment as whites.

Other speakers also stated that the equal protection clause applied generally, with the exception of denial of suffrage to blacks.[66] For example, Representative Stevens, the primary sponsor in the House, stated its purpose: "Whatever law punishes a white man for a crime shall punish the black man precisely in the same way and to the same degree. Whatever law protects the white man shall afford 'equal' protection to the black man. Whatever means of redress is afforded to one shall be afforded to all."[67] Senator Howard added that the equal protection clause "establishes equality before the law, and it gives the humblest, the poorest, the most despised of the race the same rights and the same protection before the law as it gives to the most powerful, the most wealthy or the most haughty. . . . [It] abolishes all class legislation in the States and does away with the injustice of subjecting one caste of persons to a code not applicable to the other."[68] With the exception of suffrage for blacks, which both conceded was excluded by section 2 of the fourteenth amendment, neither placed any other limit on the scope of the equal protection clause.[69] This is also consistent with the constitutional text in which the equal protection clause by its own terms applies generally and is not limited to discrimination with respect to the privileges or immunities of the first clause, let alone the specific list of rights contained in the 1866 Civil Rights Act.

Finally, when the opponents of the fourteenth amendment charged that all variety of specific racial customs and practices might be imperiled by the equal protection clause or that the privileges or immunities clause might be given a broad, open-ended construction in the future, the proponents did *not* counter as they had to such charges in the 1866 Civil Rights Act by specifying a number of practices that were not intended to be covered, deleting the broad language of the text, or providing a specific list of rights that were included.[70] For example, Representative Rogers, an opponent, complained in the House that the general scope of section 1 embraced "all the rights we have under the laws of the country" and would cover such conditions as marriage, jury service, and office-holding.[71] In the Senate, opponents complained that the broad phrases in section 1 were "vague" and "of uncertain legal meaning." Senator Johnson moved to strike the privileges or immunities clause altogether because he did "not understand what will be the effect of that" provision, but his motion was rejected out of hand. As Charles Fairman noted, this confirmed that the clause "did not have a definite meaning."[72] To the opponents' charges in the debates, the proponents responded with oratory as general as the text of section 1 itself and passed the fourteenth amendment on to the states for ratification without deleting any of the broad phrases of the text or enumerating specific rights.[73]

The congressional debates, like the text and framing of the fourteenth amendment, suggest that the meaning of section 1 was intended to be broad and open-ended. As Alexander Bickel concluded, the framers knew "that it was a *constitution* they were writing, which led to a choice of language capable of growth."[74] How its clauses would be applied in the future would depend on how subsequent constitutional decision-makers chose to interpret its meaning.[75] The congressional debates did not provide the *Plessy* and *Brown* Courts with the answer to the question of whether the equal protection clause prohibited state-mandated segregation of railroad coaches or schools.

Conclusion

Forced to make their own choice of the meaning of the equal protection clause, the *Strauder* Court, the majority and dissenting opinions in

Plessy, and the Warren Court in *Brown* all focused on the same basic questions concerning caste: Was the state act in question premised on the dominant white majority's assumption that blacks as a group belonged to an inferior class? Did it seek to relegate blacks to a subordinate caste or otherwise brand them as inherently inferior? Interpreting the equal protection clause as prohibiting such caste discrimination is consistent with the text, framing, and debates on the fourteenth amendment. This interpretation is not compelled, but it is permitted: it is well within the range of legitimate choices authorized by the Constitution.

Choosing this interpretation of the equal protection clause does not eliminate the burden of making further judicial choices in deciding the actual cases that come before the Court. Instead, the Court must also flesh out the meaning of this anticaste understanding in order to probe the evidence as it emerges in each case. In addition, only such refinement will enable the conscientious judge to evaluate the facts in order to reach a reasoned judgment as to whether the state's action is infected by caste discrimination. Although a variety of elaborations are possible,[76] consideration of the components of an anticaste principle which I have detailed elsewhere may help to explain the nature and scope of these additional judicial choices.[77]

First, the judicial inquiry examines the *process* of decision making that led to the passage and then implementation of the state act or governmentally condoned conduct in question. The focus is not on the justification for material inequalities and disproportionate outcomes between groups. Instead, the search is for a basic structural defect in the process of government, whether the official actions or refusals to act in question have been influenced by the prejudice of the majority in power against a minority group that the majority itself has singled out for abuse or disregard. This is not an easy inquiry, but a wide-ranging and sensitive search for such institutional bias in a state's official decision-making process is nevertheless required if the Court is to determine whether the ugly spectre of caste has tainted that process.

In some cases, however, the Court has expressly refused to examine the purposes underlying legislative enactments or executive actions. For example, in *Palmer v. Thompson,* the Burger Court refused to examine the motivation behind the decision of Jackson, Mississippi, to close its municipal swimming pools upon being ordered to desegregate them in compliance with *Brown.* The Court concluded that the closing of all pools affected blacks and whites equally and that the decision could not be invalidated solely because it was motivated by reason of any prejudice by the decision-makers against blacks. In support of this surprising conclusion, the Court argued first, that it is difficult to ascertain the underlying purposes of any decision; and, second, that even if the Court struck down the pool closing on finding a "bad motive," the city could turn around and make the same decision "for different reasons."[78] Both arguments miss the point.

Any difficulty in ascertaining discriminatory purpose in the decision-making process hardly justifies refusing to look for such caste-based defects altogether. Courts have regularly searched for such official discrimination in cases ranging from racial abuse of administrative discretion in systematically denying Chinese persons laundry licenses under a San Francisco ordinance neutral on its face to a state legislative scheme to redraw city boundaries to fence virtually all blacks out of Tuskegee, Alabama.[79] In *Palmer* it would have taken no genius with supersensitive racial sensors to determine whether *one* of Jackson's purposes in closing all of its municipal pools in the face of the desegregation order involved prejudice against blacks. Jackson virtually conceded this point by arguing that it closed the pools because "the City council felt they could not be operated safely and economically *on an integrated basis*." This pool closing smacks of the same Jim Crow myth of white supremacy that led the Court to strike down the antimiscegenation laws in Loving v. Virginia.[80] The irony in both is that the supposedly dominant white majority feared that any contact with the supposedly inferior black race would somehow rub off on or otherwise infect whites. Far wider-ranging proof to uncover far less overt discrimination forms the usual grist for evaluating equal protection cases, even those involving more complex claims of systemic, intentional segregation in urban schools and housing.[81]

The Burger Court's second concern is just as misplaced. Assume that Jackson would be able to close its pools for nonracist reasons after the Court invalidated the initial pool closing because it was motivated in part by white prejudice against blacks. For example, suppose Jackson did determine to close its pools five years later and defended this decision on the grounds that the pools were unsafe because they had since become contaminated due to a defect in the water supply or that there was now not enough money to run the pools on either an integrated or a segregated basis. The very first issue to be addressed by the Court is whether such ostensibly nonracial health or economic considerations actually motivated the decision or whether they were in any part just *pretexts* for seeking once again to relegate blacks to a subordinate caste. That is why the anticaste principle looks first to the *process* of decision making to determine whether it has been influenced by a majority "in-group's" prejudice against a minority "out-group" that the majority has singled out for disregard. No person or group has a constitutional right to municipal swimming pools under the equal protection clause. *Every* person has the right to a *process* of official decision making that is free from the taint of caste-based bias, including a city's determination to close the municipal swimming pools.

Second, although the white majority "in-group's" attempt to subjugate the black minority to any such subordinate caste may be the primary example of such a wrong in this country's history and a motive cause for the adoption of the fourteenth amendment in the first place, the equal protection clause is not limited by its terms to racial discrimination. Under the anticaste principle the Court does not determine in advance what minority groups are deserving of special judicial protection. Instead, the Court's evaluation begins after a state has acted or refused to act as cases are brought to the Court raising the issue; then the Court probes deeply into all relevant evidence to see whether a dominant majority in the state itself has acted to single out some group for abuse or selective neglect on the grounds that the members of this minority are inherently inferior or otherwise undeserving of personal respect and concern regardless of their individual worth.[82]

The actions of a state itself identify which, if any, group has been singled out for such caste discrimination. For example, if a state were to select Hasidic Jews, persons of Puerto Rican, German, or Japanese descent, women, or left-handers as a group to bear burdens not generally borne by others because the dominant majority in the legislature believed the group identified was inherently inferior or undeserving, the Court would be justified in finding a violation of the anticaste principle. Whites, as well as blacks, are protected under this reading of the equal protection clause from any attempt by a dominant "in-group" within a state to single any of "them" out for relegation to a second-class status.

Third, such caste discrimination is by definition a wrong committed against an entire group and, therefore, may result in wide-ranging, even systemic injury that will endure. The continuing effects of such systemic discrimination must be closely analyzed by the Court. If state acts today freeze in the effects of a previously established caste regime, then that state has failed to afford equal protection to the members of the group subordinated to an inferior position. For example, as the Court recognized in *Brown II,* merely declaring that state-mandated segregation is unconstitutional a half century after it has become the customary way of life does not relieve a state of the burden of remedying the resulting caste system. Just removing the "whites-only" and "blacks-only" signs from the schoolhouse door does not eliminate the continuing effects of the state-imposed system of segregation.[83]

The Burger Court should have evaluated Jackson's closing of municipal swimming pools from the perspective of this affirmative duty as well. For example, if official segregation pervaded community life in Jackson, the Court could have asked whether the decision to close the pools frustrated the State of Mississippi's duty to afford equal protection to all persons within its jurisdiction, including blacks living in Jackson. In response to court orders to desegregate its pools in compliance with *Brown,* the city of Jackson surely had no more discretion to perpetuate any system of Jim Crow caste than Governor Faubus in blocking the schoolhouse door in Little Rock or than the State of Virginia in closing all public schools in Prince Edward County to evade desegregation decrees.[84]

Fourth, a state as a whole is the responsible party. The equal protection clause speaks directly to the states, and it is the states that have the duty to *afford* protection from such caste-based discrimination. Under the anticaste principle, a state cannot escape this duty by compartmentalizing its responsibility and claiming that one or another of its agencies or subdivisions does not have authority over the caste discrimination in question. For example, a state does not gain immunity by claiming that it had no authority over a whites-only suburb's exclusion of blacks from its borders and containment within a central city ghetto. Nor can one agency or subdivision of a state claim that it is free to ignore the effects within its own jurisdiction that result from the caste discrimination of another subdivision or agency of the state. For example, a white suburb does not gain immunity by showing that only the acts of state and local officials from another city caused the containment of blacks within a ghetto in the center city. In both cases the issue under the anticaste principle is whether or not the racial separation results from official caste discrimination by *any* agency or office of the state. If the answer is yes, it is the state as a whole that is constitutionally responsible for affording equal protection. If the answer is no, there is *no* denial of equal protection.[85]

Similarly, a state violates its affirmative duty to afford equal protection of the laws when it closes its eyes in order to avoid consideration of the continuing effects of an established caste regime. For example, Congress enacted the 1871 Ku Klux Klan Act to enforce this equal protection duty when the former rebel states failed to protect the freedmen and their Republican allies from rule by Klan terror. Representative Perry noted, "Where these gangs of assassins show themselves, . . . sheriffs having eyes to see, see not; judges having ears to hear, hear not. . . . In the presence of these gangs all the apparatus and machinery of civil government, all the processes of justice, skulk away as if government and justice were crimes and feared detection."[86] In response to the charges of conservative opponents that such official failures to address the Klan's terror and intimidation were outside the scope of the equal protection clause, Senator Edmunds, the floor manager of the bill, cited the duties imposed directly on the states by section 1 of the fourteenth amendment and concluded, "Why, sir, if I were in any other place, I should say—'O Shame, where is thy blush.'"[87] Under the structure of the Constitution generally and the fourteenth amendment in particular, the states bear the primary duty to afford protection to all persons from such caste discrimination.

Finally, even if a state's official decision-making process is only thoughtless rather than racially malevolent, the resulting act may still operate to imply the inferiority of a minority group as a whole. Although the sting of such stigmatization may be deepened if intended, there is still a violation of the anticaste principle if the state action operates to single out a discrete group and brand it as inferior regardless of the intent of the decision makers. Such a relational injury that publicly slanders an entire group can be just as devastating as the political injury of caste-based defects in the legislative process itself. No matter how well meaning the imposition by the white majority of segregation in 1896 or in 1954, for example, there can be no question that Chief Justice Warren was right in *Brown* in finding that this "policy of separating the races is usually understood as denoting the inferiority of the Negro group" in America and therefore denied equal protection of the laws to black schoolchildren.

In contrast, there is no violation of the anticaste principle if material inequalities or disproportionate impacts that correlate with race are not the result either (1) of the political injury of caste-based defects in the official decision-making process or (2) of the relational injury of branding the minority group as inherently inferior. To understand why, consider a hypothetical community in which one side is heavily black, the other heavily white. There are no restrictions on travel or residence between the two sides. One side favors urban development, paved roads, street lights, gutters, sewers, and high taxes, while the other opts for rural scenery, natural environment, bike paths, no lights, septic tanks, and low taxes. Unless any resulting differences along racial lines can be traced to some racial bias in the communal decision-making process against the minority group or otherwise stigmatize the minority as inherently inferior, the apparent racial split may be attributed to diverse personal decisions rather than any wrongful discrimination. A new entrant to this community who is colorblind could choose his or her place of residence based on nonracial factors; and any existing member on either side could justify the material differences as the result of personal choices rather than racial exploitation. The searching inquiry into whether such differences and separation are the result of wrongful discrimination or only of personal choices is at the core of judicial review under the anticaste principle.[88]

This elaboration of an anticaste principle interprets the equal protection clause as guaranteeing the personal constitutional right of each individual in this country to be free from the continuing effects of the group wrong of caste discrimination within the states.[89] If the Justices apply this principle honestly as the facts emerge from a searching judicial inquiry, it can serve as a powerful guide in understanding the equal protection clause and living up to the meaning each chooses to read in the text of the Constitution. On the other hand, as the Court's ruling in *Plessy* demonstrates, *no* anticaste principle provides protection against caste discrimination if the Justices refuse honestly to evaluate the circumstances or choose to ignore the basic facts. In applying any anticaste principle, *no* Justice can escape the burden of judicial choice inherent in judging a case or controversy. At the very least, however, an anticaste principle does allow a future Court the opportunity to correct a prior Court's error in refusing to see the basic wrong, as in the case of state-mandated segregation, even if it does take more than fifty years for the future Court to recognize the mistake.

NOTES

1. 163 U.S. 537 (1896).
2. 347 U.S. 483 (1954).
3. 163 U.S. at 543–44 (emphasis added).
4. 163 U.S. at 544.
5. Justice Brown's citation of other state court decisions upholding school segregation and similar laws enacted by Congress to authorize segregation of the District of Columbia schools may have somewhat more relevance to his argument that segregation laws "have been generally, if not universally, recognized as within the competency of the state legislatures in the exercise of their police power." But this argument says little, if anything, about how to interpret the meaning of the equal protection clause; and Justice Brown never once suggested that the framers of the fourteenth amendment intended specifically to exclude segregation from the scope of the general equal protection guarantee contained in the text of the amendment.
6. 163 U.S. at 545. *See* Strauder v. West Virginia, 100 U.S. 303 (1880); Ex Parte Virginia, 100 U.S. 313 (1880).
7. 163 U.S. at 545.
8. 163 U.S. at 551.
9. *Id.* Expanding on this racial hypocrisy, Justice Brown added, "The [plaintiff's] argument necessarily assumes that if, as it has been more than once the case, and is not unlikely to be so again, the colored race should become the dominant power in the state legislature, and should enact a law in precisely similar terms, it would thereby relegate the white race to an inferior position. We imagine that the white race, at least, would not acquiesce in this assumption."

   Ironically, Justice Brown virtually conceded the lie in such racist sarcasm in another part of the opinion. The plaintiff, Homer Plessy, was of "mixed descent, in the proportion of seven-eighths Caucasian and one-eighth African blood" and claimed "that the mixture of colored blood was not discernible in him." Plessy therefore argued that his forced separation from the whites-only coach deprived him of his "property" interest in his reputation of belonging to the supposedly "dominant," i.e. white, race. Justice Brown countered, "Conceding this to be so, for purposes of this case, we are unable to see how this statute deprives him of, or in any way affects his right to such property. If he be a white man and assigned to a colored coach, he may have his action for damages against the [railway] company for being deprived of his so-called property. Upon the other hand, if he be a colored man and be so assigned, he has been deprived of no property since he is not lawfully entitled to the reputation of being a white man."
10. 163 U.S. at 561–62.
11. 163 U.S. at 560.
12. Justice Brown's opinion never suggested that segregation or state laws regulating railway coaches or schools were outside the scope of

relevant issues to be reviewed under the equal protection clause. Nor did he claim that equal protection of the laws was somehow limited in its scope to guarding against racially partial legislation respecting the "privileges or immunities" of all U.S. citizens, whether black or white, protected by another clause of section 1 of the fourteenth amendment. To the contrary, in an apparent bow to the Supreme Court's active supervision of state economic and social welfare regulation that would soon follow in the *Lochner* era (*see* Introduction, text at notes 20–22, supra), Justice Brown argued that *all* state legislation must be "reasonable" in order to pass constitutional muster under the fourteenth amendment: "every exercise of the [state's] police power must be reasonable, and extend only to such laws as are enacted in good faith for the promotion of the public good, and not for the annoyance or oppression of a particular class." In the *Plessy* Court's view, however, Louisiana's segregation law was not "unreasonable" given the "established [racial] usages, customs, and traditions of the people," such as the "acts of Congress requiring separate schools for colored children in the District of Columbia . . . or the corresponding acts of state legislatures."

13. 163 U.S. at 559.
14. In 1903 in Giles v. Harris, 189 U.S. 475, the Supreme Court allowed the states to finish the stage set for the complete subjugation of blacks to a subordinate caste. The Court concluded that it lacked the judicial power to interfere with Alabama's disfranchisement, in direct violation of the fifteenth amendment, of black voters. The Court remitted the plaintiff, Jackson Giles, as it had Homer Plessy, to state court for a possible damage action. Money, of course, would not be any substitute for the denial of the right to vote to the millions of blacks who had voted previously and otherwise would continue to vote in local, state, and national elections. Within a decade after *Giles,* the states succeeded in excluding virtually all blacks from the polls on election day and fencing them out of the process of representative democracy altogether. Jackson Giles, like Homer Plessy before him, would not receive any monetary damages in state court as the price for this unconstitutional denial of the vote. *See* Giles v. Teasley, 193 U.S. 146 (1904); and Dimond, *The Anti-Caste Principle,* 30 WAYNE L. REV. 1, 19–20 and n.57 (1983).
15. *See, generally,* W.E.B. DUBOIS, THE SOULS OF BLACK FOLK (1903); G. MYRDAL, AN AMERICAN DILEMMA (1944), C. V. WOODWARD, THE STRANGE CAREER OF JIM CROW (1957).
16. 347 U.S. at 489.
17. 345 U.S. 972.
18. 49–49a LANDMARK BRIEFS AND ARGUMENTS OF THE SUPREME COURT (P. Kurland and G. Caspar eds. 1975).
19. *See* R. KLUGER, SIMPLE JUSTICE (1976).
20. 347 U.S. at 489.
21. *Id.*
22. 347 U.S. at 490, citing *Strauder, supra* note 6.
23. 347 U.S. at 491.
24. 347 U.S. at 492.
25. 347 U.S. at 492.
26. 347 U.S. at 492.
27. 347 U.S. at 492.
28. 347 U.S. at 494. In support of this conclusion, the Chief Justice cited

a number of studies by eminent psychologists and sociologists. Such evidence understandably had been presented in the lower courts as part of the attack on the *Plessy* Court's claim that any implications of inferiority arose solely because blacks chose to put that construction upon it. For the Chief Justice to rely on such "new" studies from the "science of social psychology," however, detracted from the force of Warren's moral argument that segregation was wrong, harmful to human beings, and part and parcel of an official system designed to relegate blacks to a subordinate caste because of the white majority's assumption of black inferiority. It also opened the Warren Court to the unnecessary criticism that it was just substituting its own popular psychology of the moment for the racial hypocrisy of the *Plessy* Court.

29. 347 U.S. at 494.
30. 349 U.S. 294, 300–01 (1955).
31. 163 U.S. at 557.
32. *See, generally,* R. BERGER, GOVERNMENT BY JUDICIARY (1977).
33. *See,* J. TENBROEK, THE ANTISLAVERY ORIGINS OF THE FOURTEENTH AMENDMENT (1951); Graham, *The Early Antislavery Background of the Fourteenth Amendment* (pts. 1–2), 1950 WIS. L. REV. 479, 610.
34. Even if the framers who proposed the amendment all agreed on a code meaning for the general phrasing used in the text of the amendment, two interpretive problems remain. First, this specific code meaning may have little relevance unless it was also generally understood and agreed to by those in the state legislatures who ratified the amendment. How one is to prove from the scanty historical materials on ratification that there was such a secret compact is difficult to imagine. Second, the plausibility of such an agreement as to a code meaning by the diverse consituencies represented in the state legislatures ratifying an amendment is equally troublesome. After all, it is the text itself that is actually adopted as an amendment to the Constitution. In interpreting an amendment, are we nevertheless bound to infer some dark or abstruse, shadow meaning from the quite different sense conveyed by the words of the text itself? If the framers intended a different meaning from that contained in the text itself, they could have written the provision differently.
35. *See* Introduction, *supra,* text at note 19.
36. Section 2 of article IV provides: "The Citizens of each State shall be entitled to all Privileges and Immunities of Citizens in the several States." This clause had not been the subject of much interpretation by the Supreme Court prior to the framing of the fourteenth amendment. By its terms, however, it applied to rights guaranteed or provided by the states, not to national rights as in the privileges or immunities clause of section 1 of the fourteenth amendment. It has been understood only as a comity provision assuring, for example, that one state does not discriminate against nonresident visitors with respect to the important privileges it chooses to grant its own residents.
37. The phrase "due process of law" may also have had some substantive connotation at the time of the framing of the fourteenth amendment. In particular, as the so-called police powers of government gradually expanded to regulate

more and more aspects of commerce and everyday life, those individuals and businesses affected challenged the regulation as beyond the power of the governmental unit in question. In weighing these claims, some courts used the term "due process of law" as a general substantive limit on the exercise and expansion of the police power. *See* Wynehammer v. People, 13 N.Y. 378 (1856); W. LOCKHART, Y. KAMISAR, & J. CHOPER, CONSTITUTIONAL LAW 425–27 (1980). Given the availability of the privileges or immunities clause to protect any national substantive rights as against the states, it seems unnecessary to read the due process clause as applying to anything more than the fair process its language describes.

38. *See* Dimond, *Strict Construction and Judicial Review of Racial Discrimination under the Equal Protection Clause,* 80 MICH. L. REV. 462, 465–68 (1982).
39. Howard, *Laws in Relation to the Freedmen,* 1 S. EXEC. Doc. No. 6, 39th Cong., 2d Sess. 170–230 (1867).
40. *See, e.g., id.* at 170–71, 180–81, 181–83, 184–85, 186, 218–19, 229–30.
41. Quoted in E. MCPHERSON, THE POLITICAL HISTORY OF THE UNITED STATES OF AMERICA DURING THE PERIOD OF RECONSTRUCTION 42 (1871). *See also* REPORT OF THE JOINT COMMITTEE ON RECONSTRUCTION, 39th Cong., 1st Sess. Part II, 2, 55, 83, 235–36, Part III, 9, 22, 36, 71, Part IV, 56, 69, 82 (1866); REPORT OF GENERAL CARL SCHURZ ON THE STATES OF SOUTH CAROLINA, GEORGIA, ALABAMA, MISSISSIPPI, AND LOUISIANA, 1 S. EXEC. Doc. No. 2, 39th Cong., 1st Sess. 22, 24–25, 82 (1865).
42. The enumerated list was expressed as follows: ". . . citizens, of every race and color, without regard to any previous condition of servitude . . . shall have the same right, in every State and Territory in the United States, to make and enforce contracts, to sue, be parties and give evidence, to inherit, purchase, lease, sell, hold and convey property, and to the full and equal benefit of all laws and proceedings for the security of person and property, as is enjoyed by white citizens, and shall be subject to like punishment, pains, and penalties, and to none other, any law, statute, ordinance, regulation, or custom to the contrary notwithstanding."
43. CONG. GLOBE, 39th Cong., 1st Sess. 211–12 (1866).
44. *See, e.g.,* CONG. GLOBE, 39th Cong., 1st Sess. 322, 457, 477–78, 599, 606, 1117.
45. *See* JOURNAL OF THE JOINT COMMITTEE OF FIFTEEN ON RECONSTRUCTION 46 (B. Kendrick ed. 1914); Dimond, *supra* note 38, at 486–87.
46. *See, e.g.,* CONG. GLOBE, 39th Cong., 1st Sess. 103, 1088 (1866).
47. In 1856, Bingham had opposed the power of the territorial legislatures to abridge such rights on the grounds that natural law, the Declaration of Independence, the preamble to the Constitution, the provisions guaranteeing a Republican form of government, the Bill of Rights, and implicitly "equal protection" all prohibited such laws, despite the lack of any supporting Supreme Court authority. *See* CONG. GLOBE. 34th Cong., 1st Sess., App. 122–26 (1856) & 3d Sess. App. 135–40 (1857). This rhetoric, advanced in opposition to the spread of slavery, was not unique; it was included in the Re-

publican platform of 1856. *See* 1 NATIONAL PARTY PLATFORMS 27 (D. Johnson ed. 1978). Thereafter, Bingham repeatedly challenged the *Dred Scott* Court's ruling that blacks were inferior beings without any rights or privileges under the Constitution. He claimed that each state had the obligation to provide "due protection" of all "natural rights" (although he did concede that suffrage for blacks was not such a right, even while praising Massachussets for allowing blacks to vote because "political rights are inseparable from manhood and citizenship, and in no wise dependent upon complexion or the accident of birth"). *See, e.g.*, CONG. GLOBE, 35th Cong., 1st Sess. 399–402, 1864–66 (1858), 2d Sess. 981–85 (1859); 36th Cong., 2d Sess., App. 82–84 (1861); and 37th Cong., 2d Sess. 1638–40 (1862).

48. CONG. GLOBE, 39th Cong., 1st Sess. 1093 (1866).
49. *Id.*
50. *See, e.g.*, CONG. GLOBE, 39th Cong., 1st Sess. 1089–90 (1866).
51. CONG. GLOBE, 39th Cong., 1st Sess. 1095 (1866).
52. CONG. GLOBE, 39th Cong., 1st Sess. 1291–93 (1866).
53. CONG. GLOBE, 39th Cong., 1st Sess. 1291 (1866).
54. *Id.*
55. CONG. GLOBE, 39th Cong., 1st Sess. 1367, 1861 (1866); Dimond, *supra* note 38, at 490 and nn. 146–47.
56. JOURNAL OF THE JOINT COMMITTEE, *supra* note 45, at 83–120.
57. "The want of the Republic today is not a Democratic Party, is not a Republican Party, is not any party save a party for the Union, for the Constitution, for the restoration of all the States to their political rights and powers under such irrevocable guarantees as will forevermore secure the safety of the Republic, the equality of the States, and the equal rights of all the people under the sanctions of inviolable law." He added that section 1 would "protect by national law the privileges and immunities of all the citizens of the Republic and the inborn rights of every person within its jurisdiction whenever the same shall be abridged or denied by the unconstitutional acts of any State," including, for example, state imposition of "cruel and unusual punishments." Bingham also claimed, "No State ever had the right, under the forms of law or otherwise, to deny to any freeman the equal protection of the laws or to abridge the privileges or immunities of any citizen of the Republic, although many of them have assumed and exercised the power, and that without any remedy." CONG. GLOBE, 39th Cong., 1st Sess. 2542 (1866).
58. CONG. GLOBE, 39th Cong., 1st Sess. 2542 (1866).
59. Given his rhetorical flair, structured view of federalism, and not altogether precise thinking, it may not be surprising that widely divergent meanings have been read into Bingham's performance in framing the fourteenth amendment and opposing the 1866 Civil Rights Act. For example, Raoul Berger argues that Bingham was a believer in "State's Rights" whose opposition to the 1866 Civil Rights Act confirms the narrowest conceivable reading of section 1 of the fourteenth amendment. *See* R. BERGER, GOVERNMENT BY JUDICIARY 119–23 (1976). In contrast, tenBroek and Graham see Bingham as the vessel through which flowed the broadest conceivable natural rights philosophies of the

evangelical abolitionists. *See* J. TENBROEK, THE ANTISLAVERY ORIGINS OF THE FOURTEENTH AMENDMENT 125–28 (1951); Graham, *The Early Antislavery Backgrounds of the Fourteenth Amendment,* 1950 WIS. L. REV. 610. Charles Fairman expressed his own frustration with Bingham by labeling him "an ardent rhetorician, not a man of exact knowledge or clear conceptions or accurate language." C. FAIRMAN, RECONSTRUCTION AND REUNION 1864–88 (Pt. 1) (6 HISTORY OF THE SUPREME COURT) 462 (1971). Such wildly differing views of the man make it difficult to perceive how Bingham ever could have framed section 1 of the fourteenth amendment as a code for some specific set of rights that he expressed clearly to others or to which others could expressly agree.

60. *See* Dimond, *supra* note 38, at 494–502 for a more detailed discussion of the debates in Congress on section 1.
61. C. FAIRMAN, RECONSTRUCTION AND REUNION 1283 (1971).
62. *See, e.g.,* CONG. GLOBE., 39th Cong., 1st Sess. 2459 (Rep. Stevens), 2461 (Rep. Finck), 2462 (Rep. Garfield), 2498 (Rep. Broomall), 2512–13 (Rep. Raymond), 2505 (Rep. Wilson), and 2961 (Sen. Poland) (1866).
63. *See, e.g.,* J. ELY, DEMOCRACY AND DISTRUST at 198–200 n. 66; (1980); A. BICKEL, THE LEAST DANGEROUS BRANCH 101–05 (1962); C. FAIRMAN, *supra* note 61, at 1387–88; Bickel, *The Original Understanding and the Segregation Decision,* 69 HARV. L. REV. 1, 59–63; and Dimond, *supra* note 38 at 496–97. *But see* R. BERGER, GOVERNMENT BY JUDICIARY (1977).
64. *See, e.g.,* CONG. GLOBE, 39th Cong., 1st Sess. 2542 (Rep. Bingham), 2765–66 (Sen. Howard), 2461 Sen. Poland. *Cf. id.* at 3039–40 (Sen. Hendricks), 3041 (Sen. Johnson) (opponents) (1866).
65. CONG. GLOBE, 39th Cong., 1st Sess. 2765–66 (1866). Raoul Berger nevertheless argues that the privileges or immunities clause was somehow understood by the framers in Congress as having a quite different shadow or code meaning, namely the narrowest conceivable reading of the specific list of rights enumerated in the 1866 Civil Rights Act. He also complains that any more general reading of the text of the clause would amount to "playing a trick upon an unsuspecting people" in the ratification process. R. BERGER, GOVERNMENT BY JUDICIARY 107 (1977); *see also id.,* at 57, 105, 112. I have refuted Berger's myopic reading of the debates elsewhere, primarily with respect to the scope of the equal protection clause. *See* Dimond, *Strict Construction and Judicial Review of Equal Protection under the Equal Protection Clause,* 80 MICH. L. REV. 462 (1982). With respect to the privileges or immunities clause, John Ely's evaluation of Berger's claims will suffice: "[Berger] puts the matter upside down. . . . Obtaining ratification of open-ended language in the expectation that it will be given an open-ended interpretation is not playing a trick. Trickery would inhere in gaining ratification of facially specific language and then giving it a [broad] construction, or equally—and this is the methodology favored by Berger—in gaining ratification of open-ended language and then forever limiting its reach to the particular recorded

[examples provided by] the Congress that proposed it to the States." J. ELY, DEMOCRACY AND DISTRUST 30, 200 n.69 (1980). *See also* A. BICKEL, THE LEAST DANGEROUS BRANCH 102–03 (1962).

66. *See, e.g.*, CONG. GLOBE 39th Cong., 1st Sess. 2459 (Rep. Stevens), 2462 (Rep. Garfield), 2510 (Rep. Miller) 2539 (Rep. Farnsworth), 2542 (Rep. Bingham), and 2766 (Sen. Howard), 2964 (Sen. Stewart), 3035 (Sen. Johnson), 3037 (Sen. Yates), app. 219–20 (Sen. Howe) (1866).
67. *Id.* at 2459.
68. *Id.* at 2766.
69. School segregation was never mentioned directly in the congressional debates on the fourteenth amendment. The subject came up only once, and only obliquely at that, when Senator Howe, a supporter of the amendment, explained in a rambling discourse that section 1 was aimed generally at unequal laws such as the Black Codes. One of the codes that he mocked as a "crime" was a Florida law that provided that taxes from white and black taxpayers would support whites-only schools, while taxes from only black taxpayers would support blacks-only schools. CONG. GLOBE, 39th Cong., 1st Sess. App. 218–19 (1866).
70. CONG. GLOBE, 39th Cong., 1st Sess. 2467 (Rep. Boyer), 2538 (Rep. Rogers), 3090–40 (Sen. Hendricks), 3145–46 (Rep. Finck), 3147 (Rep. Harding), app. 230 (Rep. Rogers), app. 242–43 (Rep. Davis) (1866). *See also* Dimond, *supra* note 38, at 497, 501.
71. CONG GLOBE, 39th Cong., 1st Sess. 2538 (1866).
72. *Id.* at 3039–40 (Sen. Hendricks), 3041 (Sen. Johnson). *See also* C. FAIRMAN, *supra* note 61, at 1297.
73. Such generality in the supporting rhetoric is hardly surprising. Not only was it consistent with the breadth of phrasing used in the text of the proposed amendment, it also served to incite the least political controversy and to engender the most support in the states. Perhaps an example of the political problems arising once the proponents of a proposed amendment allow the debate to sink to the specific may be helpful. The recent proposal for an Equal Rights Amendment to prohibit discrimination based on sex was in serious trouble the minute the debate turned to such specifics as whether it would prohibit, for example, sex-segregated bathrooms in public facilities or males-only combat rules during wartime.
74. Bickel, *supra* note 63, at 63. *See also* A. BICKEL, *supra* note 63, at 102–03; C. FAIRMAN, *supra* note 61, at 1387–88; Fairman, *The Attack on the Segregation Cases*, 70 HARV. L. REV. 83, 86–87 (1956).
75. The Congress continued to argue over the reach of section 1 for the next ten years, as it debated and passed a series of civil rights acts under its enforcement authority conferred by the thirteenth, fourteenth, and fifteenth amendments. *See, e.g.*, Dimond, *supra* note 38, at 478–81, 502–07. Although the Republicans did not succeed in specifically outlawing every practice of public and private racial discrimination imaginable, they did go a surprisingly long way. And even when they did not succeed, the particular legislation did not fail because it fell outside the potential reach of section 1 but because it remained outside Congress's grasp at the time. For example, bills to outlaw all segregation in the newly forming public schools did not pass. In their final

consideration during the debates and framing of the 1875 Civil Rights Act, conflicting provisions either to outlaw all school segregation or specifically to authorize separate but equal schooling were hotly contested. In the end, a compromise was reached by which both provisions were dropped and no mention of schools was made in the 1875 Civil Rights Act as finally enacted. Representative Monroe explained the basis for this compromise: blacks were willing "to take their chances under the Constitution and its amendments" rather than consent to the "discrimination" inherent in the separate but equal schooling proposal. 3 CONG. REC. 997 (1875). In the text, framing, and debates on the fourteenth amendment and in the ensuing inaction on segregated schools, Congress left the issue of the constitutionality of public school segregation open for decision under the equal protection clause.

76. *See, e.g.*, J. ELY, DEMOCRACY AND DISTRUST (1980); Brest, *In Defense of the Anti-Discrimination Principle,* 90 HARV. L. REV. 1 (1976); Fiss, *Groups and the Equal Protection Clause,* 5 PHIL. AND PUB. AFFAIRS 107 (1976); Perry, *The Disproportionate Impact Theory of Racial Discrimination,* 125 U. PA. L. REV. 540 (1977).
77. *See* Dimond, *The Anti-Caste Principle,* 30 WAYNE L. REV. 1 (1983); Dimond, *Provisional Review,* 12 HASTINGS CONST. L.Q. 201, 218–20, 222 n.82, 226, 237–38 (1985); Dimond & Sperling, *Of Cultural Determinism and the Limits of Law,* 83 MICH. L. REV. 1065, 1077–80, 1083–86 (1985). *See also,* L. TRIBE, AMERICAN CONSTITUTIONAL LAW 1515–21 (1988) ("anti-subjugation principle").
78. Palmer v. Thompson, 403 U.S. 217, 224–25 (1971).
79. Yick Wo v. Hopkins, 118 U.S. 356 (1886); Gomillion v. Lightfoot, 364 U.S. 339 (1967).
80. 388 U.S. 1 (1967).
81. *See, generally,* P. DIMOND, BEYOND BUSING (1985); Dimond, *The Anti-Caste Principle,* 30 WAYNE L. REV. 1 (1983).
82. In Personnel Administrator v. Feeney, 442 U.S. 256 (1979), the Burger Court failed to evaluate whether a state's preference for veterans in its civil service amounted to a pretext for caste discrimination against women. In the case, there was no dispute that the preference had a discriminatory impact: 47 percent of the men in the state over eighteen were veterans compared to less than 1 percent of the women. In evaluating whether the state's decision to retain the veteran's preference was influenced at all by a purpose to keep women in a subordinate status, the Court refused to evaluate the prior incarnations of the preference with any sensitivity and concluded "nothing in the record demonstrates that this preference for veterans was originally devised or subsequently reenacted because it would accomplish the collateral goal of keeping women in a stereotypic and predefined place in the [state] civil service." In dissent, Justice Marshall retorted that this conclusion "displays a singularly myopic view of the facts. . . ." In particular, "until 1971, the statute and implementing civil service regulations exempted from operation of the preference any job requisitions 'especially calling for women.' In practice, this exemption, coupled with the absolute preference for veterans [in other positions], has created a gender-based civil service

hierarchy, with women occupying low grade clerical and secretarial jobs and men holding more responsible and remunerative positions." That surely amounted to strong evidence that the state's preference for veterans was openly influenced through 1971 by the type of caste assumption that led the Supreme Court in 1873 to uphold a state law denying women the right to practice law: "Man is, or should be woman's protector and defender. . . . [T]he natural and proper timidity and delicacy which belongs to the female sex evidently unfits it for many of the occupations of civil life. [The] paramount destiny and mission of woman are to fulfill the noble and benign offices of wife and mother. This is the law of the Creator." Bradwell v. Illinois, 83 U.S. 130, 141 (1873). The Court majority in *Feeney* therefore did not sensitively review the facts to see whether the state's continuation of the veteran's preference after 1971 without the exemption for "woman's work" was a pretext in any part for keeping women in such a subordinate caste.

83. *See, e.g.*, Green v. County School Board, 391 U.S. 430 (1968); Dimond, *supra* note 77, 30 WAYNE L. REV. at 25–27. Ely's particular elaboration of how the Constitution protects against caste-based defects in the legislative process makes no mention of any affirmative remedial component. This may be due to his focus on explaining a theory of *initial* violation in the official decision-making process. See J. ELY, DEMOCRACY AND DISTRUST 135–79 (1980). Having invalidated a particular legislative act or administrative action because invidious "we-they" distinctions infected the decision-making process, Ely apparently leaves the members of groups thereby harmed to hang on the discretion of the offending decision makers for any relief. While this may be appropriate if such defects in official decision making are only isolated instances, it surely doesn't meet the state's duty to provide equal protection to all persons where a state has succeeded by dint of decades of sustained effort to relegate members of the selected minority group to a subordinate caste. *See* Dimond, *The Anti-Caste Principle,* 30 WAYNE L. REV. 1 (1983); Dimond & Sperling, *Of Cultural Determinism and the Limits of Law,* 83 MICH L. REV. 1065 (1985).
84. Cooper v. Aaron, 358 U.S. 1 (1958); Griffin v. County School Board, 377 U.S. 218 (1964).
85. Days, *School Desegregation in the 1980's,* as YALE L.J. 1737, 1753–68 (1986); Dimond, *supra* note 77, at 6.
86. CONG. GLOBE, 42nd Cong., 1st sess., app. 78–80 (1871).
87. *Id.*, at 697.
88. *See, e.g.*, Dimond, 30 WAYNE L. REV. 1, 8–10 (1983); Dimond & Sperling, *Of Cultural Determinism and the Limits of Law,* 83 MICH. L. REV. 1065, 1068–69, 1076–80, 1083–86 (1985).
89. The extent to which the anticaste principle applies, if at all, to the national law-making process of Congress and to the other acts of the federal government will be explored in chapter 5.

CHAPTER 2 Resolution of Federal-State Conflicts: Understanding Congressional Supremacy and the Provisional Role of the Court

Chapter 1 illustrated how the Constitution does not give the Supreme Court the answer to all cases or controversies that come before it. Instead, the Constitution often authorizes the Court itself to make a choice among a range of alternatives and to elaborate the reasons for that choice. In interpreting the meaning of section 1 of the fourteenth amendment, for example, the Court may substitute its judgment for the policy embodied in a law enacted by the elected representatives of the people in the several state legislatures. If the Court's judgment is viewed as the final word, judicial review by an unelected Court appears to conflict with the first principle of representative democracy, that government requires the consent of those governed as expressed by the laws enacted by a majority of the people's duly elected representatives.

This chapter therefore explores whether the structure of the Constitution offers any insights into how to resolve this apparent dilemma. The relationship between the Congress, the Court, and the states provides the key. The structure of the Constitution may be read as granting the Court power to overturn state laws that the Court finds in conflict with federal interests, but as vesting Congress with final authority to resolve such federal-state frictions. Such an approach frees the Court to act much as a common law court in resolving such tensions of federalism in the first instance based on the Court's independent evaluation of the merits of the issues. Consistent with the first principle of representative democracy, however, the people through their elected representatives in Congress retain the final say in how to resolve any federal-state conflict, even after the Court has first spoken. First we will explore how the Court has generally chosen to read the Constitution as providing just such a provisional approach to judicial review of federal-state conflicts, and then we will examine how section 1 of the fourteenth amendment may be read to fit into the same framework of provisional review.

Provisional Review of Federal-State Conflicts

Chief Justice John Marshall's opinion for the Court in *McCulloch v. Maryland* provides the starting point.[1] In 1816 Congress incorporated, for the second time, a national bank of the United States. Several states responded by prohibiting the bank from operating within their jurisdictions altogether or by imposing heavy taxes against any bank not chartered by the state. Maryland responded by making it unlawful for any bank not established by the state to issue notes without payment of an annual tax of 2 percent of the face value of the notes. McCulloch, the cashier of the Baltimore branch of the national bank, issued federal bank notes without paying this tax; Maryland sued and prevailed in state court. On review in the Supreme Court of the United States, Maryland argued, first, that Congress lacked the power under section 8 of Article I of the Constitution to charter the national bank and, second, that Maryland had the power under the Constitution to impose the tax on the bank's notes in any event. After hearing nine days of oral argument, Chief Justice Marshall issued the opinion for the Court only three days later.

As to the *first* issue, Marshall ruled that Congress had the power under section 8 of article I to incorporate the national bank. He concluded that section 8 vested Congress with the authority to use any means rationally related to the ends encompassed within the powers therein enumerated, unless expressly prohibited elsewhere in the Constitution.[2] In Marshall's words, "Let the end be legitimate, let it be within the scope of [section 8. Then] . . . all means [which] are appropriate, which are . . . adapted to that end [and] which are not prohibited, . . . are constitutional."[3] Subject to restraints imposed by the Constitution external to section 8 (such as the Bill of Rights),[4] Congress may select "any means adapted to [the] end" within the enumerated powers of Congress.[5] As section 8 enumerated the power of Congress "to lay and collect taxes; to borrow money; to regulate commerce; to declare and conduct a war; and to raise and support armies and navies," Chief Justice Marshall ruled that Congress was free to choose the means of a national bank to assist in implementing these "great powers."[6]

Maryland nevertheless argued that the necessary and proper clause of section 8 should be read to restrict the means which Congress could employ to implement its enumerated powers.[7] Maryland's claim reflected Thomas Jefferson's opposition as Secretary of State to the first national bank in 1790–91: Congress should be limited to using means or exercising implied powers only to the extent *necessary* and *indispensable* rather than merely *convenient* to the exercise of the enumerated power; otherwise, Congress would have the power to "swallow up" all powers and the sovereignty reserved to the states.[8] Chief Justice Marshall responded by choosing instead to read the "necessary and proper clause" not as any such limit, but as a confirmation of his understanding of the broad implied powers entrusted to Congress to implement its "great powers" enumerated in section 8. Marshall added, "where the law is not prohibited [by any restriction external to section 8], and is really calculated to effect any of the objects entrusted to the [national] government, to undertake here [in the Supreme Court] to inquire into the degree of [the law's] necessity would be to pass the line which circumscribes the judicial department, and to tread on legislative ground. This court disclaims all pretensions to such a power."[9]

Maryland claimed that Congress did violate one constitutional limit external to section 8, that imposed by the tenth amendment.[10] Marshall chose to read this particular limitation, however, as a tautology: if the congressional act represented a rational means to implement the enumerated powers, then it was within the powers "delegated to the United States by the Constitution" and therefore was *not* "reserved to the States respectively, or to the people" under the tenth amendment. By contrasting the Articles of Confederation, which provided that "each state retains [every] power [not] *expressly* delegated" to Congress, Marshall argued that any state sovereignty limit on congressional power would therefore have "to depend on a fair construction of the whole" text and structure of the Constitution.[11] As Marshall chose to read the implied powers of Congress under a rational relationship test and refused to have the Court engage in any review of the necessity of the means chosen, he read the Constitution as giving Congress the power virtually to "swallow up" the States.[12]

Marshall made this choice because of his understanding that the *people* adopted the Constitution and thereby vested "great powers" in the national government. Maryland and the other states had not by grace ceded a few specific powers to a confederation and reserved the vast remainder to the sovereign states.[13] Although Marshall was not unmindful of the resulting delicacy of the relations between the federal government and the states, he determined that it was not for the Court to exercise its awesome power of judicial review as the final arbiter under *Marbury* to tell the Congress when it had somehow transgressed the will of the people in interfering with the states. That was an issue to be decided not by unelected Supreme Court Justices for all time, but by the people's own representatives in Congress whenever they wished.

Chief Justice Marshall based this interpretive choice on his understanding of the relationship between the Congress, the states and the Court under the structure of the Constitution as a whole in creating a representative democracy within a federal system. In particular, "[i]n the legislature of the Union alone . . . are all [of the people from all of the states] represented."[14] Indeed, "the people of all of the states, and [hence] the states themselves, are represented in Congress, and, by their representatives, exercise [the enumerated federal] power."[15] Marshall concluded, "The legislature of the Union alone, therefore, can be *trusted* by the people with the power of controlling measures which concern all, in the confidence that it will not be abused."[16]

With a few exceptions,[17] the Court has since adhered to this understanding of the structure of the Constitution in deferring to congressional determinations of the extent to which federal power should be exercised despite any claim that the federal law usurps sovereign power reserved to the states. The modern Court, for example, has not acted as a final arbiter in reviewing congressional action under the commerce clause to determine whether regulation of activity within the states affects interstate commerce or should be reserved solely for regulation by the states. Instead, the Court has deferred to congressional exercise of the power under article I "to regulate commerce . . . among the several States."

Consider cases like *Heart of Atlanta Motel, Inc. v. United States*[18] and *Katzenbach v. McClung.*[19] In the Public Accommodations Section of the 1964 Civil Rights Act, Congress had outlawed discrimination on grounds of race, color, religion, or national origin in all establishments open to the public, including motels and restaurants. In *McClung* the Court upheld the application of the act under the commerce clause to Ollie's Barbecue, a family-owned restaurant in Birmingham, Alabama, that refused to serve black patrons. In *Heart of Atlanta* the Court upheld the act as applied to a local motel in Atlanta, Georgia, that refused to accommodate black guests.

In both cases the whites-only establishments claimed that their exclusion of black patrons had no significant impact on interstate commerce and that their activities were so local in nature that their regulation should be reserved to the states. The Court refused to be drawn into reviewing the extent of the impact upon commerce of the particular motel or restaurant: for example, the sale of ketchup by all of the Ollie's Barbecues of the country might effect national commerce, and the exclusion of blacks by such restaurants might have "an adverse impact on the free flow of interstate commerce." It was enough for the Court that "Congress had a rational basis for finding that [the evil attacked by Congress] affected commerce" and that "the means it selected [including total prohibition] are reasonable and appropriate."[20] Consistent with Chief Justice Marshall's understanding of the structure of our federal system and the role of the Court under the Constitution in *McCulloch,* the Court has chosen to read the Constitution as generally entrusting Congress, which represents the people from all of the states, with the power finally to resolve virtually all federal-state conflicts. This is true even in those cases involving issues of morality, public health, and/or safety that should guide the conduct of all of the people within the states and even all of the activities of the states themselves.[21]

As to the *second* issue, Maryland's claim that it retained the power to tax the national bank even if Congress had the power to incorporate the bank, Chief Justice Marshall relied on the *same* line of reasoning to strike down the state tax. In contrast to the trust that could be placed in Congress to represent the interests of all of the people from all of the states, the national interest was not represented at all in the Maryland legislature. The only ones protected against abuse of Maryland's power to tax were the state's own constitutents who elected the state legislature.

Federal interests were obviously no more represented in Maryland's elective process than the residents of other states. In this sense, Maryland's tax on the national bank just amounted to another form of taxation without representation.

The proof of the discrimination imposed by Maryland against those not represented in its legislature was evident in the tax at issue. Rather than a uniform tax on the real property of the bank in common with all other real property in the state, for example, Maryland singled out only the notes issued by the national bank for taxation because this federal institution was not chartered by Maryland. When a state thereby seeks to single out or otherwise to interfere with the constitutional operations of the federal government, "it acts upon institutions created, not by [the state's] own constituents, but by people over whom [the state] claims no control. It acts upon the measures of a government created by others as well as [the state itself], for the benefit of others in common with the [state's own constituents]."[22] The State of Maryland therefore could not be *trusted* to represent the interests of the federal government and its instrumentalities and agents,[23] and the Court ruled Maryland's tax on the national bank unconstitutional under the supremacy clause.[24]

This holding of unconstitutionality, however, was binding as the final word only against Maryland and all of the other states that were trying to tax, to hamstring, or otherwise to scuttle the national bank. Under *McCulloch,* Congress retained the enumerated powers to close the national bank itself or to authorize the states to tax or otherwise to regulate the national bank. Chief Justice Marshall chose to interpret the structure of the Constitution as vesting this ultimate power over federal-state conflicts in Congress, the only legislature in which all of the people from all of the states are represented under the Constitution. This reading authorizes the Court in the first instance to strike down state laws that impact national interests that are not represented in state legislatures. But it vests final authority over such federalism issues in the Congress.

Since *McCulloch,* the Court has followed this provisional approach to judicial review of federal-state conflicts in a variety of contexts, including, for example, state regulation of goods, vehicles, commerce, and persons that impacts the flow of commerce and people between the states; state discrimination against federal officials, instrumentalities, and interests and nonresidents within a state; state assertion of extraterritorial jurisdiction; state taxation of nonresident persons and corporations; state disputes with other states; and state regulation of rivers, lakes, and the air.[25] In the first instance, the Court itself evaluates the federal-state conflict, both in defining the federal interest and weighing it against the conflicting state policy. The Court bases its rulings in these cases on a variety of sources, including (1) federal common law generated by the Court itself, (2) judicial interpretation of a constitutional federal statute that the Court finds in conflict with state regulation, or (3) the Court's interpretation of the constitutional text (e.g., the commerce clause in article I, the privileges and immunities and full faith and credit clauses in article IV, or the structure of the Constitution as a whole) as establishing federal interests that need to be protected against state regulation. Whatever the source chosen by the Court to resolve the federal-state conflict initially, the court will then defer to any alternative that Congress enacts to resolve the federal-state conflict in a different manner, so long as the act does not violate any other limit imposed on all congressional power elsewhere in the Constitution.[26]

Consistent with the national, representation-reenforcing choices made by Chief Justice Marshall in *McCulloch*, this establishes the basic framework for provisional review of federal-state conflicts under the Constitution. In the first instance, the Court develops, evolves, and applies policies over time, much as a common law court, to resolve federal-state conflicts as they come before the Court in a variety of cases and controversies. The Court's rulings bind the states, but they are not final. The people, through their representatives in Congress, are empowered by the Constitution to legislate alternative policies any time they wish, so long as this national lawmaking process does not violate any of the other restrictions placed on Congress elsewhere in the Constitution.[27] In enacting its alternative choices, of course, Congress is free to substitute a different national policy binding on all of the states *or* to authorize the states to legislate their own policies. So long as the Court does not choose finally to hamstring Congress in the name of preserving state sovereignty, the people have the power through appropriate national legislation to allocate more or less power to, or to share concurrent power between, the federal government and the states.

In all of these cases, in sum, the Court acts as the available neutral national forum to initiate a dialogue with the people, through their duly elected national representatives, as to whether state policy conflicts with the Court's interpretation of federal interest under the Constitution. But the Court's vision of these federal limits on state power is subject to revision by the Congress.

Provisional Review of Conflicts between Section 1 of the Fourteenth Amendment and the States

While the Bill of Rights placed restrictions only on the federal government, section 1 of the fourteenth amendment imposed national limits on state power. A spate of civil rights acts and expansions of federal court jurisdiction enacted thereafter during Reconstruction served to "interpose the federal courts between the States and the people, as the guardians of the people's federal rights."[28] Read in this context, judicial interpretation of section 1 of the fourteenth amendment can therefore be understood as another of the sources by which the Court in the first instance may choose to resolve conflicts between the states and federal interests, in this case the individual's national rights as set forth in section 1 itself against the states.

By its terms, section 1 binds only the states and does not even purport to limit the federal government. As a result, unless some other provision of the Constitution imposes the same limits on federal power, the Congress may respond to the Court's interpretation of section 1 by exercising its enumerated powers under section 8 of article I to enact alternative national policies to bind the states. In short, the relationship of judicial interpretation of section 1 of the fourteenth amendment to congressional power under article I may be read to fit perfectly within the structure for provisional review of all other types of federal-state conflicts.

This reading, however, does not fit with the common wisdom, sometimes given lip service, that the Court must always have the final say on the meaning of the Constitution. From this viewpoint, the Court's declaration of national rights under section 1 of the fourteenth amendment should, *somehow,* bind the Congress as well as the states. For example, the Court has developed a "ratchet" theory to interpret congressional enforcement power under section 5.[29] Under this approach, the Congress supposedly may exercise its power under section 5 of the fourteenth amendment only to "enforce" rights guaranteed by section 1, but not to "dilute," "define," or to "reverse" these rights.[30] Although a plausible interpretive choice, this attempt to read internal limits on congressional power into the text of section 5 itself smacks of the same sort of definitional game of active review that Chief Justice Marshall rejected in *McCulloch* and that the Modern Court rejected beginning in 1937.[31] After all, the enforcement power enumerated in section 5 can also be read as an affirmative grant of power, as much as the commerce clause or the necessary and proper clause in section 8 of article I, to which the Court ordinarily applies a deferential, rational basis standard of review.[32]

Just as telling, even if section 5 is interpreted restrictively as granting Congress only limited enforcement powers, section 5 does *not* by its terms restrict in any way the other powers of Congress enumerated, for example, in section 8 of article I. These powers are more than sufficient to allow Congress to establish national policies, including personal rights, that bind the states.[33] Under this reading of the basic structure of the Constitution, the Court then reviews the exercise of congressional power enacting alternative national policies not against its own interpretation of the meaning of section 1 of the fourteenth amendment, but against the restrictions that the Constitution does place on Congress, such as the Bill of Rights.

Some of the commentators argue that the Bill of Rights should be read by the Court to impose the same restrictions on Congress as the Court interprets section 1 of the fourteenth amendment as imposing on the states.[34] The irony in this argument is that it calls for a reverse form of incorporation, that the Bill of Rights somehow incorporates section 1 of the fourteenth amendment, while the full Court has never even accepted the argument that section 1 of the fourteenth amendment fully incorporates the Bill of Rights.[35] Given the substantial difference in the text and purposes of section 1 of the fourteenth amendment as compared to the ten amendments that form the Bill of Rights, such a reading is surely not compelled.

For purposes of analysis, therefore, assume that the Bill of Rights does not incorporate the fourteenth amendment. Chapters 3 through 7 will explore the nature and extent of the limits that the Bill of Rights does impose on Congress. It is sufficient for now to suspend judgment as to what limits the Constitution imposes on Congress. This will permit analysis, first, of the nature and extent of the Court's ability to use section 1 of the fourteenth amendment to resolve conflicts between the states and claimed national rights and, second, of the scope of congressional power to enact a different national policy to govern these disputes.

The Court may use a variety of sources to interpret the meaning of section 1 of the fourteenth amendment as creating national rights that limit state power. The primary sources, of course, are the text and syntax of the amendment. As set forth in chapter 1, both suggest that the privileges or immunities clause may be read as a rather open-ended invitation to articulate national rights, while the due process clause may be interpreted to cover fair procedures and the equal protection clause to protect against caste discrimination.[36] The framing and legislative history of the debates in Congress also support this reading.[37] This understanding of the due process and equal protection clauses relates primarily to fair process in the making and enforcement of law by the states. As a result, it reinforces representational values consistent with democracy. Equal protection and due process can be read as limiting the *manner* by which the state enacts and enforces its policies consistent with representative democracy, but not as restricting the ultimate substance of state decisions concerning the allocation of resources, moral values, human aspirations, and costs and benefits.[38]

In contrast, the privileges or immunities clause is an open-ended invitation to the Court to define, in the first instance, those fundamental national rights of membership in the national community that may also bind the substance of state law. As John Ely notes, this clause is "a delegation to future constitutional decision-makers" to declare and to protect national rights against the states that the Constitution "neither lists, at least not exhaustively, nor even in any specific way gives directions for finding."[39] Although this reading of the privileges or immunities clause is not compelled, it is authorized.[40]

Ely argues that one of the reasons that the Court has not chosen to embrace this reading since the more limited interpretation provided by a five-man majority in the *Slaughter-House Cases*[41] "has to be that the invitation extended by the language is frightening. . . ."[42] The irony, of course, is that the Court has chosen to stretch to find just such an "invitation" in the due process clause of the fourteenth amendment, whose language fits more easily into a fair process limit on state action.[43] In either case, Ely challenges those who choose to read section 1 of the fourteenth amendment as inviting the Court to impose open-ended restrictions on the substance of state decisions in the name of national rights: "If a principled approach to judicial enforcement of the Constitution's open-ended provisions cannot be developed, one that is not hopelessly inconsistent with our nation's commitment to representative democracy, responsible commentators must seriously consider the possibility that courts should stay away from them."[44]

This challenge is met *if* the Court's interpretations of section 1 of the fourteenth amendment are understood as provisional judgments of national rights binding on the states, subject to revision by Congress enacting different national policies pursuant to its enumerated powers under section 8 of article I. Under the structure of provisional review, the Court accepts the open-ended invitation of the text of section 1 of the fourteenth amendment by interpreting its language much as a common law court in positing national rights that the states must respect, until revised by a law enacted by Congress in which all of the people are represented. Even Ely concedes that such a "common law" approach to interpreting national rights does not really conflict with the nation's commitment to representative democracy.[45]

This understanding of the provisional nature of judicial review under section 1 of the fourteenth amendment makes the open-ended invitation of the language of the privileges or immunities clause considerably less frightening. The Court's interpretation of that clause merely initiates a dialogue with the people, through their representatives in Congress, as to what national rights of individuals should bind the states.[46] It thereby frees the Court to look to a variety of sources for interpreting substantive national rights. These sources may include, for example, other provisions of the Constitution (such as the Bill of Rights), the federal structure of the Constitution as a whole, evolving national values, the laws enacted by the states and the common law created by state courts concerning personal rights, the minimum that is required in each generation to be a member of the national community, the evolving balance between individual autonomy and state power.

There is nothing wrong in having the Court, as a neutral national forum which is at least somewhat insulated from the heated political passions of the moment, address such critical substantive issues. The only danger to representative democracy arises if the Court's answers are viewed as forever final rather than as the initial positions in an ongoing national dialogue that Congress is generally empowered to resolve.

Consider, for example, a state prohibition against any member of the armed services voting in state elections on the ground that such military personnel are too transient to have sufficient connection with that state to be deemed residents. The Court under provisional review might well look to the structure of the Constitution as interpreted in *McCulloch* and invalidate this state act under section 1 of the fourteenth amendment because it imposes undue burdens on members of the national community who are serving their nation. Similarly, consider cases involving one state that prohibits any in-migration on the ground that the state can't support any more people and another state that prohibits out-migration on the ground that it can't afford to lose any population. The Court might strike down both state acts as violating a national privilege of each person to move freely about the nation.[47]

As other examples, consider one state that bars any attendance at private schools on the ground that the public schools are losing the support of the public and another state that prohibits the teaching of any foreign language in any school on the ground that it interferes with learning the state's official language of English. The Court might invalidate both of these statutes because they interfere with a national privilege of the family and of the individual to choose for themselves where they want to be educated and how they want to learn. Or consider state statutes that prohibit any person from reading *Lady Chatterly's Lover* or from viewing a hedonistic movie, even in the privacy of one's home, because they endanger the character and morals of the people. The Court might invalidate both statutes on the ground that they interfere with a citizen's national immunity from state laws that infringe on what a person wants to read, think, or watch in the privacy of his or her own home. Or consider state laws that seek to prohibit demonstrations against the state motto and require adherence to a particular religious faith. The Court might invalidate such state statutes because they conflict with the privilege of members of the national community to freedom of personal conscience and with their immunity from state establishment of any religion.[48]

The point of these examples is not to argue that the substantive reasons for the Court's decisions are the most persuasive that can be imagined, but that they are plausible initial attempts to develop a common law of national rights. By evaluating the substance of the arguable individual rights and of the state interests in conflict, the Court's resolution may serve to raise the issues for debate in an ongoing national dialogue. Over time, the Court will itself respond to the merits of this debate as the nation's values and the Court's own thinking evolve; but the people, subject only to the limitations imposed on all congressional exercises of enumerated powers elsewhere in the Constitution, are free to legislate a different national policy.

Conclusion

Authorizing an unelected Court to create national rights as a common law court and to strike down the acts of states under section 1 of the fourteenth amendment may seem to invite judicial usurpation of what little sovereignty Chief Justice Marshall's interpretation of the Constitution in *McCulloch* may have left to the states. But there are safeguards for the states. First, they have the opportunity to persuade the Court that their substantive reasons for enacting or enforcing a particular law outweigh any national rights the individual may claim. Second, they have the opportunity to persuade the Court that the claimed national right or interest should not be credited. Third, they have the opportunity to persuade the Court that, even if there is a conflict between the state policy and the claimed national right, that the states should be given some leeway to solve the issue for themselves. Each of these points can be made by the states to the neutral national forum that, over the years, has not been unmindful of the real interests of the states nor overly enthusiastic in creating and protecting national rights.

Whatever the Court's reaction to these arguments by the states, there is under provisional review a final political failsafe for the states—the Congress in which the people from all of the states are represented. Far from being an unsympathetic forum, Congress is made up of representatives elected by the people from each of the states. The congressional embrace of decentralized programs of "new federalism" (e.g., to substitute block grants and revenue sharing for specific entitlement programs) provides a recent example of the responsiveness of Congress to the states' interest in their own discretion in determining how to govern themselves.[49]

Provisional review, moreover, specifically authorizes Congress to enact laws empowering the states to legislate their own answers. In the national dialogue over what it means to be a member of the national community, Congress is not limited to substituting a different substantive policy for that initially offered by the Court. Congress may also legislate to return the decision on the merits of the issues to the states, as it has already done on numerous occasions.[50]

Thus, any concern that provisional review will strip the states of their sovereignty or of their ability to function effectively in a federal system is misplaced. As in *McCulloch*, provisional review of federal-state conflicts leaves the states free to use the political safeguards of representative democracy under our federal system to overturn or to modify the Court's initial resolution in order to secure national deference to state interests. In contrast, if the fourteenth amendment is interpreted as giving the Court final authority over such federal-state conflicts, the states can only turn to the extraordinarily difficult route of constitutional amendment to secure support for state discretion. In weighing the relative risks of provisional review for the states and the individual, therefore, the greater danger may be faced by individuals who find that their judicially declared national rights under section 1 of the fourteenth amendment are subject to revision by ordinary legislation enacted by Congress. If provisional review creates the opportunity for the Court to stimulate national dialogue over the meaning of the Constitution, it also invites Congress through ordinary legislation to override the Court and the judicially declared national rights of the individual.

The Constitution, however, does impose limits on all congressional power. Perhaps, the most important may be found in the Bill of Rights. With respect to these restrictions, the Court has the duty of judicial review under *Marbury* to determine in an appropriate case or controversy whether Congress has acted unconstitutionally. The nature and scope of the restrictions that the Court chooses to interpret the Bill of Rights as imposing on Congress will therefore determine the shape of the national dialogue over the meaning of the Constitution and the extent to which provisional review ultimately protects the rights of the individual and minorities from tyranny by the majority in our representative democracy.

NOTES

1. 17 U.S. (4 Wheat.) 316 (1819).
2. 17 U.S. at 415, 419, 421, 423. *See also* L. TRIBE, AMERICAN CONSTITUTIONAL LAW 300–05 (1988).
3. 17 U.S. at 421.
4. Section 9 of article I provides the other prime source of such external restraints imposed by the Constitution on any exercise of the powers of Congress enumerated in section 8. The nature and extent of these external limits on the national lawmaking powers are canvassed in considerable detail in chapters 4–7. *See also* L. TRIBE, AMERICAN CONSTITUTIONAL LAW 297 (1988).
5. 17 U.S. at 419.
6. 17 U.S. at 407–11.
7. Clause 18 of section 8 provides: "The Congress shall have the power . . . to make all Laws which shall be necessary and proper for carrying into execution the foregoing Powers [enumerated in clauses 1–17], and all other Powers vested by the Constitution in the Government of the United States, or in any Department or Officer thereof."
8. Alexander Hamilton, the Secretary of the Treasury at the time, had argued that Congress had the implied power to use any means that bore a natural relation to the lawful ends enumerated in the Constitution. *See generally*, G. GUNTHER, CONSTITUTIONAL LAW 83–87 (1985). The irony for contemporary politics in this debate over the first national bank is that the conservative Hamilton argued for national power, while the liberal Jefferson argued for states' rights.
9. 17 U.S. at 423. *Cf. also* Gibbons v. Ogden, 22 U.S. (9 Wheat.) 1 (1824) (Chief Justice Marshall's opinion for the Court choosing to apply this same conception of the judicial role in reviewing congressional power under the commerce clause).
10. The tenth amendment provides: "The powers not delegated to the United States by the Constitution, nor prohibited by it to the States, are reserved to the States respectively, or to the people."
11. 17 U.S. at 406.
12. Indeed, in the years following the Civil War, Congress exercised its

enumerated powers by excluding the former rebel states from representation in Congress altogether and by establishing military districts to govern these areas of insurrection. With a push from Congress after oral argument in a case challenging the constitutionality of this virtually total federal displacement of these states, the Court chose to duck the issue altogether. *See* Ex Parte McCardle, 74 U.S. (7 Wall.) 506 (1869); G. GUNTHER, CONSTITUTIONAL LAW 40–42 (1985).

13. 17 U.S. at 402–05.
14. 17 U.S. at 431.
15. 17 U.S. at 435.
16. 17 U.S. at 431.
17. In the *Lochner* era, for example, the Court disregarded Marshall's teachings and actively reviewed whether every congressional exercise of power was necessary in view of its impingement on state sovereignty. *See* Hammer v. Dagenhart, 247 U.S. 251 (1918) (striking down the federal act that excluded products of child labor from interstate commerce because the law invaded state police powers); Carter v. Carter Coal Company, 298 U.S. 238 (1936) (striking down the federal statute regulating the wages and hours of mine workers because the Court said local labor relations had too indirect an effect on interstate commerce and congressional regulation would therefore usurp the authority of the states over their domestic concerns). These decisions were also couched in terms of internal limits on enumerated powers the *Lochner* era Court inferred from the text of section 8 itself. For example, the Court read the commerce clause as restricting the reach of congressional power to situations in which there was a direct and substantial effect on interstate commerce. This limiting construction just dragged the Court back into the very policy determinations of "necessity" that Chief Justice Marshall held in *McCulloch* were the province of Congress and not the Court. Beginning in 1937 the modern Court began to take shape by returning to Chief Justice Marshall's considered judgment to trust the Congress to be the people's elected representative—rather than the unelected Court—with the final authority to resolve such federal-state tensions. *See* NLRB v. Jones & Laughlin Steel Corp., 301 U.S. 1 (1937) (upholding federal intervention in labor relations); and U.S. v. Darby, 312 U.S. 100 (1941) (upholding federal regulation of wages and hours of employment in local manufacturing).

    For a brief period and in only one case, William Rehnquist, at that time an associate justice, again disregarded Marshall's teachings in leading a divided Court to strike down a federal law regulating the wages and hours of employees of state and local governments. Although conceding that the act was within Congress's enumerated powers under section 8 of article I, Rehnquist nevertheless concluded that the act was a violation of the sovereignty that he chose to read the tenth amendment as reserving to the states. *See* National League of Cities v. Usery, 426 U.S. 833 (1976). Although Rehnquist continued to pitch his interpretive choice in subsequent cases in order to have the Court itself weigh the national interest against state sovereignty, his balance favoring the states was rejected in each subsequent case; finally, his active judicial review as a final arbiter of such federal-state conflicts was explicitly overruled in Garcia v. San Antonio Metropolitan Transit Auth., 469 U.S. 528 (1985). *See* Dimond, *Provisional Review,* 12 HASTINGS CONST. L.Q. 201, 213–15 (1985). As Justice Blackman reiterated for the Court in *Garcia,* "the principal means chosen by the Framers to ensure the role of the States in the federal system lies in the structure of the Federal Government itself. . . . State sovereign interests, then, are more properly protected by procedural safeguards [, primarily "through State participation" in the "national political process,"] inherent in the structure of the federal system than by judicially created limitations on federal power."

18. 379 U.S. 241 (1964).
19. 379 U.S. 294 (1964).
20. 379 U.S. at 258.
21. In addition to the public accommodation cases cited in text, *see* Champion v. Ames (Lottery Case), 188 U.S. 321 (1903); Fitzpatrick v. Bitzer, 427 U.S. 445 (1976); Garcia v. San Antonio Metropolitan Transit Auth., 469 U.S. 528 (1985); and, generally, W. LOCKHART, et al., CONSTITUTIONAL LAW 107–08, 142–55 (1980).
22. 17 U.S. at 435.
23. 17 U.S. at 425–37.
24. The supremacy clause of article VI provides: "The Constitution, and the Laws of the United States which shall be made in Pursuance thereof . . . shall be the supreme Law of the Land; and the Judges in every State shall be bound thereby, any Thing in the Constitution or Laws of any State to the Contrary notwithstanding." Once again, note that Marshall's reading of the supremacy clause as invalidating state laws that conflict with the Court's understanding of the federal interest may be authorized, but it is not compelled. Marshall made a choice in reading the supremacy clause, just as he made choices in interpreting (1) section 8 of article I as granting broad implied powers to Congress, (2) the necessary and proper clause as a confirmation of this generous interpretation rather than as a sharp restriction on the means that could be used in implementing all of the enumerated powers, and (3) the tenth amendment as no restriction on congressional action within its enumerated powers. Each of Marshall's choices, however, vests the Congress, and not the Court, with the final authority over all such issues. As a result, no one can quarrel with Marshall's interpretation of the Constitution on the ground that it conflicts in any way with representative democracy. To the contrary, it is the aberrant choices made in *Hammer* during the *Lochner* era and in *National League of Cities* under Rehnquist (*see* note 17 *supra*) that smack of judicial activism run amuck, precisely because they are at war with the basic principles of representative democracy.
25. *See, e.g.,* J. CHOPER, JUDICIAL REVIEW AND THE NATIONAL POLITICAL PROCESS 205–09 (1980); C. BLACK, STRUCTURE AND RELATIONSHIP IN CONSTITUTIONAL LAW 13–20 (1969); L. TRIBE, AMERICAN CONSTITUTIONAL LAW 401–545 (1978); Abrams & Dimond, *Toward a Constitutional Framework for the Control of State Court Jurisdiction,* 69 MINN. L. REV. 75,

85–95 (1984); Dimond, *Provisional Review,* 12 Hastings Const. L.Q. 201, 209–15 (1985); Dowling, *Interstate Commerce and State Power,* 27 Va. L. Rev. 1 (1940); Monaghan, *Constitutional Common Law,* 89 Harv. L. Rev. 1, 13–17 (1975); Sedler, *The Negative Commerce Clause as a Restriction on State Regulation,* 31 Wayne L. Rev. 885 (1985); Wechsler, *The Political Safeguards of Federalism,* 54 Col. L. Rev. 543 (1954). *Also* Leisy v. Hardin, 135 U.S. 100 (1890); Hinderlider v. La Plata River & Cherry Creek Ditch Co., 304 U.S. 92 (1938); Southern Pac. Co. v. Arizona, 325 U.S. 761, 768–80 (1945); Dean Milk Co. v. Madison, 340 U.S. 349 (1951); Carrington v. Rash, 380 U.S. 89 (1965); Pike v. Bruce Church, Inc., 397 U.S. 137, 142 (1970); City of Milwaukee v. Illinois, 406 U.S. 91 (1972); Hicklin v. Orbeck, 437 U.S. 518 (1978); Zobel v. Williams, 457 U.S. 55 (1982); Kassel v. Consolidated Freightways Corp., 450 U.S. 662 (1981); McCarty v. McCarty, 453 U.S. 210 (1981).

26. *See* note 25 *supra. Also* Pennsylvania v. Wheeling and Belmont Bridge Co., 59 U.S. 421 (1855); In re Rahrer, 140 U.S. 55 (1891); City of Milwaukee v. Illinois, 451 U.S. 301 (1981); 14 U.S.C. 1408 (overriding Court's prior ruling in *McCarty, supra,* concerning division of military pension in state court divorce proceedings); and 28 U.S.C. 1738A (overriding Court's rulings under full faith and credit clause concerning state court custody proceedings).
27. The nature and extent of these external limits imposed by the Constitution on all national lawmaking, including congressional resolution of federal-state conflicts, will be explored in chapters 3 and 4.
28. Mitchum v. Foster, 407 U.S. 225, 242 (1975).
29. Section 5 of the fourteenth amendment provides: "The Congress shall have the power to enforce, by appropriate legislation, the provisions of this [amendment]."
30. *See* Katzenbach v. Morgan, 384 U.S. 641, 651 n.10 (1966); Oregon v. Mitchell, 400 U.S. 112 (1970), supplanted by the twenty-first amendment.
31. *See* discussion *supra,* text at notes 9–17.
32. *See* discussion *supra,* text at notes 6 and 18–21; *also* L. Tribe, American Constitutional Law 348–50 (1988).
33. *See* discussion *supra,* text at notes 18–21 and 25–26.
34. *See* L. Tribe, American Constitutional Law 350 and n. 98 (1978); Cohen, *Congressional Power to Interpret Due Process and Equal Protection,* 27 Stan. L. Rev. 603 (1975).
35. *See* J. Ely, Democracy and Distrust 24–28 (1980); W. Lockhart et al., Constitutional Law 480–97 (1980); Fairman, *Does the Fourteenth Amendment Incorporate the Bill of Rights?,* 2 Stan. L. Rev. 5 (1949).
36. *See* discussion chapter 1 *supra,* text at notes 35–38.
37. *See* discussion chapter 1 *supra,* text at notes 39–74.
38. *See* J. Ely, Democracy and Distrust (1980).
39. J. Ely, Democracy and Distrust 28 (1980). *See also id.* at 30; C. Fairman, Reconstruction and Reunion 1297, 1387–88 (1971); Kurland, *The Privileges or Immunities Clause,* 1972 Wash. U.L.Q. 405.

40. This interpretation of the privileges or immunities clause therefore bridges the conflicting claims of interpretivist and noninterpretivist theories of judicial review. *See* discussion, Introduction, *supra*. Both must confront this clause's authorization for the Court, in deciding cases that come before it, to look for norms that are nowhere specifically defined or listed in the Constitution itself. How the Court should respond to this express invitation is a judicial choice that neither can avoid.
41. 83 U.S. 76 (1873). *See also* discussion *supra*, Introduction, at note 63.
42. J. Ely, Democracy and Distrust 23 (1980).
43. *See* discussion *supra*, Introduction, text at and notes 17–22 and 63.
44. J. Ely, Democracy and Distrust 41 (1980).
45. *Id.*, 187 n.13.
46. By its terms the privileges or immunities clause prohibits any state from making or enforcing any law abridging "the privileges or immunities of citizens of the United States." Ely argues that this phrasing should be interpreted to describe a category of national rights that the states may not deny to anyone, whether the victim is a citizen or an alien. J. Ely, Democracy and Distrust 25 (1980). An alternative approach that may be more responsive to the federal structure of the Constitution would interpret the clause as protecting only citizens and use two other sources to protect aliens. First, under the anticaste principle of the equal protection clause, which by its terms applies to all persons, the Court could examine the process by which a state seeks to distinguish between citizens and aliens to determine if naked prejudice—rather than relevant differences between citizens and aliens—influenced the decision. *See* chapter 1 *supra*. Second, under the structure of the Constitution, the Court could determine that the state regulation of aliens in question should be decided by Congress under its enumerated powers over immigration and nationalization. *See* the discussion of Provisional Review of Federal-State Conflicts, *supra* text at notes 1–26. In either case, the Court's decision would suspend the state's classification against aliens until Congress acts pursuant to its enumerated powers under section 8 of article I to impose the same condition, to authorize the states to pass such a regulation, or to establish other conditions for aliens.
47. *Cf.* C. Black, Structure and Relationship in Constitutional Law (1969); Carrington v. Rash, 386 U.S. 89 (1965); Edwards v. California, 314 U.S. 160 (1941).
48. *Cf.* Meyer v. Nebraska, 262 U.S. 390 (1923); Pierce v. Society of Sisters, 268 U.S. 510 (1925); Stanley v. Georgia, 394 U.S. 557 (1969); Wooley v. Maynard, 430 U.S. 705 (1977); West Virginia State Board of Education v. Barnette, 319 U.S. 624 (1943).
49. *See also, e.g.*, congressional authorization on a retroactive basis of state division of military pensions in divorce settlements following the Supreme Court's ruling that such state actions interfered with congressional attempts to protect military pensions (14 U.S.C. 1408, overriding McCarty v. McCarty, 453 U.S. 210 (1981)); congressional authorization of state liquor regulation (In re Rahrer, 140 U.S. 545 (1891)), previously ruled im-

permissible by the Court (Leisy v. Hardin, 135 U.S. 100 (1890)); and congressional redefinition of state discretion in regulating the lengths of semi-trucks (Pub. L. 97-369, 96 Stat. 1765 (1983)) after the Court hamstrung the states (Kassel v. Consolidated Freightways Corp., 450 U.S. 662 (1981)).

50. *See* note 49 *supra;* and Cohen, *Congressional Power to Validate Unconstitutional State Laws,* 35 STAN. L. REV. 387 (1983).

CHAPTER 3 The Bill of Rights and Congressional Power: Completing the Structure for Provisional Review

Chapter 2 demonstrated that the Constitution may be interpreted as vesting Congress generally with the enumerated power to resolve state versus federal conflicts. The Court often provides a neutral national forum to referee such disputes in the first instance, whether based on an interpretation of the federal interest generally under the structure of the Constitution as a whole or of the national rights of individuals specifically under section 1 of the fourteenth amendment. Unless constrained by some other aspect of the Constitution, Congress may then exercise its enumerated powers to enact the policy preference of its choice. This basic constitutional structure provides the framework for provisional review.

Such national legislation is not, however, necessarily free from judicial review by the Supreme Court. Although Congress is in no way bound by section 1 of the fourteenth amendment, its acts are subject to the external limits imposed, for example, by the Bill of Rights on *all* national legislation. How the Court chooses to interpret these limits on congressional power will determine the extent to which Congress may substitute its policy preferences for those of the Court in determining the national rights of individuals that the states must continue to respect.[1] How the Court chooses to interpret these limits will also shape the nature of the dialogue between the people, through their representatives in Congress, and the Court over the meaning of the Constitution.

Substantive Limits

The Constitution may be interpreted as imposing a relatively few types of restrictions on the *substantive* reach of this congressional lawmaking power. For example, consider cases in which the Court in the first instance rules that state laws establishing Christianity as the official state religion or prohibiting the worship of Buddha, authorizing the state militia at any time to be quartered in any person's house, requiring random searches of houses for criminal conduct by their residents, paying $1 to condemn a person's home for use as public library, or mandating death as the punishment for stealing a loaf of bread "abridge the privileges or immunities of citizens of the United States" in violation of section 1 of the fourteenth amendment. Acting within its enumerated powers to override the Court's policy judgment by authorizing or requiring the states to establish such substantive policies, the Congress is nevertheless constrained by the first, third, fourth, fifth, and eighth amendments. As a result, the Court could review such congressional legislation and rule it unconstitutional as violating the prohibitions of the first amendment against Congress making any "law respecting an establishment of religion, or prohibiting the free exercise thereof," of the third amendment against quartering any soldier "in time of peace in any house without the consent of the owner," of the fourth amendment "against unreasonable searches and seizures," of the fifth amendment against taking "private property for a public use, without just compensation," and of the eighth amendment against inflicting "cruel and unusual punishments."

Although each of these prohibitions may also serve the purpose of preventing those in control of government from picking on their opponents, each serves more than the purpose of procedural fairness: important substantive values are also protected. The Bill of Rights may be read by the Court as fencing Congress out of making laws that infringe these substantive values, just as much as the Court in *Marbury* read section 2 of article III as prohibiting Congress from expanding the original jurisdiction of the Supreme Court itself. With respect to the interpretation of these substantive restrictions on congressional law-making power, the dialogue between the people and the Court over the meaning of the Constitution therefore must be conducted through the process of discourse, public pressure, new legislation, new appointments to the Court, case-by-case adjudication, and constitutional amendment that has by now become familiar. Compared to the potential sweep of the national privileges or immunities that the Court might in the first instance declare as binding against the states under section 1 of the fourteenth amendment, however, the substantive restrictions that the Bill of Rights places on Congress can be interpreted by the Court as relatively narrow.[2]

Process Restrictions

That does not mean, however, that the process by which Congress chooses to substitute its policy preferences for those of the Court in defining other national rights of citizens as against the states is free from review by the Court. Such national legislation is subject to the same restraints as the Court interprets the Constitution as imposing on any exercise by Congress of its enumerated powers.

The Supreme Court's review of the congressional law-making process may be divided into three main categories: first, what John Ely calls representation-reinforcing values,[3] such as free speech and assembly, and fair apportionment in the House of Representatives; second, anticaste limits on the process of national lawmaking;[4] and, third, a requirement that the Congress decide the merits of the issues in a visible fashion when legislating in areas that implicate important constitutional interests. The Court may choose to use these three judicial techniques to shape the process by which Congress makes law and, thereby, the dialogue with the people over the meaning of the Constitution.

Representation-Reinforcing Values

The first amendment provides "Congress shall make no law . . . abridging the freedom of speech, or of the press; or the right of the people peaceably to assemble, and to petition the Government for a redress of grievances." Whatever more expansive reading some may choose to give the first amendment with respect to any personal rights of self-expression and autonomy,[5] the first amendment can be read at least as operating to prohibit Congress from abridging *political* expression, assembly, and protest, which are essential for self-government in a representative democracy.[6]

As John Ely notes, the Court "must police inhibitions on expression and other political activity because we cannot trust elected officials to do so: ins have a way of wanting to make sure the outs stay out."[7] To assist in this difficult task, the Court has developed two approaches to review of first amendment claims. First, any law that is aimed at the content of speech is unconstitutional per se. Second, any law that clogs up a channel of communication without regard to the content of speech must be weighed against the alternative means of communication available and the interests served by the regulation in question.[8] Together, these two approaches may help the Court assure that our elected representatives neither jam the means of political discourse to prevent consideration of alternative points of view nor single out any political opposition for silencing.[9]

The first amendment's protection of political expression from abridgment by Congress provides only part of the foundation necessary for the operation of a representative democracy. The people must also be able to elect the representatives who will govern them. Section 2 of article I provides, "The House of Representatives shall be composed of Members chosen every second year by the people of the several States. . . ."[10] With the exception of the discounts for slave persons provided in section 2 from the outset and for blacks denied the right to vote after the passage of the fourteenth amendment, article I further provides that the number of representatives "shall be apportioned among the several States . . . according to their respective numbers . . . of . . . persons. . . ."

In *Wesberry v. Sanders*,[11] the Warren Court chose to interpret these provisions as requiring "one person-one vote" in apportioning the congressional districts *within* each state: ". . . as nearly as practicable one man's vote in a congressional election is to be worth as much as another's." Justice Black, writing for the Court, argued that, "To say that a vote is worth more in one district than in another would not only run counter to our fundamental ideas of democratic government; it would cast aside the principle of a House of Representatives elected 'by the people' . . . ."[12] Given the administrative difficulty for the Court in enforcing virtually any other standard to assure that one person's vote is not unconscionably diluted compared to that of another, the Court chose the "one person–one vote" standard as the prophylactic means to guarantee that the people could hold their elected representatives accountable by having their right to vote to replace them at the next election mean something for *each* voter.[13]

In choosing to protect both political debate and the right of each voter meaningfully to participate in influencing the outcome of congressional elections from abridgement, the Court interprets the Constitution so as to reinforce the representative nature of the national political process. That gives all persons *some* confidence that the national process of lawmaking can be trusted (1) not to silence the voices of any of the people and (2) to be representative of the majority will of the people, not only in levying taxes and distributing funds for the general welfare, in declaring wars and regulating commerce among the states, and in borrowing and coining money, but also in declaring what national rights of individuals the states must respect. It provides the opportunity for the people, through their discussion of issues and election of representatives, to continually debate the merits and come to different conclusions over time. It provides *some* assurance that the people will respect the laws enacted by the Congress because they have the opportunity not only to consent to those national laws with which they agree but also to seek changes with those laws with which they disagree.

The Anticaste Principle

The Court's choice to interpret the Constitution as imposing such representation-reinforcing values on the national political process is influenced by the desire to make sure that no group in control of Congress is able systematically to skew the process of representative democracy so as to single out a group not in power or an idea not in favor for official disregard forever. As discussed in chapter 2, the equal protection clause of the fourteenth amendment can be interpreted to serve a similar function: to assure that, no matter how representative the political process and open the public debate, no majority "in-group" within any state will be permitted to identify a minority "out-group" and relegate its members to an inferior caste. The problem is that there is *no* equal protection clause that similarly binds Congress and the national lawmaking process.

John Ely notes this difficulty in criticizing the Warren Court's ruling in *Bolling v. Sharp*, the companion case to *Brown*, that the segregation of the District of Columbia public schools violates the due process clause of the fifth amendment.[14] Ely argues, "It's hard to see how" the due process clause of the fifth amendment "incorporates" the prohibitions of the equal protection clause of the fourteenth amendment. Chief Justice Warren in his opinion for the Court, however, made *no* such assertion. Instead, he explicitly recognized that the fifth amendment does "not contain an equal protection clause as does the fourteenth amendment which applies only to the States." He then continued, "But the concepts of equal protection and due process, both stemming from the American ideal of fairness, are not mutually exclusive. The 'equal protection of the laws' is a more explicit safeguard of prohibited unfairness than 'due process of law,' and, therefore, we do not imply that the two are always interchangeable phrases. But . . . discrimination may be so unjustifiable as to be violative of due process." Warren's standard of "fairness" for the process of national as well as state lawmaking surely amounts to something akin to the antidiscrimination value that flows from Ely's own articulation of representation-reinforcing review. The Chief Justice concluded by holding that "Segregation in public education is not reasonably related to any proper governmental objective, and thus it imposes on Negro children of the District of Columbia a burden that constitutes an arbitrary deprivation of their liberty in violation of the due process clause."[15]

Ely's criticism of *Bolling* is even more peculiar because Ely relies on similar reasoning in explaining why the due process clause of the fifth amendment includes such an antidiscrimination component. After explaining a hypothetical case in which a national official selects three of his six subordinates for an "especially hazardous assignment" out of hostility toward those singled out, Ely argues: "It is inconsistent with constitutional norms to select people for unusual deprivation . . . because the official doing the choosing doesn't like them. When such a [purposefully discriminatory] principle of selection has been employed, the system has malfunctioned: indeed we can accurately label such a selection a denial of due process."[16] In support of this reasoning, Ely quotes the ruling in *Department of Agriculture v. Moreno* that a "bare congressional desire to harm a politically unpopular group cannot constitute a legitimate governmental interest."[17] Perhaps Chief Justice Warren was not as direct in his statement of why federal authorization of segregation in the District of Columbia schools amounted to just such a violation of the fair process due in the national lawmaking process under the fifth amendment, but he surely made much the same point.

There remains a difficult interpretive question: even if due process of law can be understood as prohibiting such caste-based defects in the national lawmaking process, how does such discrimination deprive a person of the particular objects of the due process protection, namely life, liberty, and property? How does the undue process inhering in a congressional decision to segregate the District of Columbia public schools deprive the schoolchild of "liberty" or "property"? John Ely does not address this issue at all. Chief Justice Warren in *Bolling* attempted to answer the question by arguing that liberty "extends to the full range of conduct which the individual is free to pursue, and it cannot be restricted except for a proper governmental objective."[18] The problem with this suggestion is that it implies that some liberty interest akin to freedom of association may be at work here. But that associational principle is not the basis for either *Brown* or *Bolling*: in these segregation cases the schooling was compulsory not voluntary, and the constitutional wrong related to the entire *system* of segregation by which the white majority sought to relegate the black minority to a subordinate caste, not to any associational rights.[19]

There are, however, plausible alternative answers. For example, if public education in the District of Columbia schools is an entitlement granted by the national government, then it does represent a "property" interest which Congress may not deprive without due process in its lawmaking. The caste restrictions on the schoolchildren's enjoyment of this entitlement can then be understood as "depriving" them of their "property, without due process of law." Similarly, if personal reputation is viewed as "property," then the white majority's official slander in Jim Crow segregation statutes of blacks as inherently inferior also amounts to a "deprivation" of "property, without due process of law." This social or relational injury is, after all, one of the two major types of violations of the anticaste principle.[20]

There is also a more direct way of understanding how the national government's imposition of segregation violates due process whether or not any property interest is deemed to be deprived. Liberty can be interpreted as including the right to be free from just such caste-based defects in the national lawmaking process; and such caste discrimination is totally at odds with the process of law due in a representative democracy under our Constitution. This political injury of prejudice infecting the official decision-making process is, of course, the other major type of violation of the anticaste principle.[21] As such, *all* actions of the federal government may be subject to review under the due process clause of the fifth amendment for such deprivations of liberty in the official decision-making process, whether or not they are also deemed to deprive anyone of property.[22]

In his insightful dissent in *Korematsu v. United States,* Justice Murphy made just this point with respect even to the enumerated powers of Congress to declare and the President to conduct war. He argued that the forced removal of Japanese Americans from the West Coast and their internment in camps inland during World War II could only be justified "upon the assumption that *all* persons of Japanese ancestry may have a tendency to commit sabotage and espionage. . . ." To Justice Murphy, this assumption was based on racial prejudice by the white majority against Japanese Americans without regard to the loyalty or disloyalty of the individuals forcibly removed *en masse* from the Pacific Coast. Additional proof of this gross racial defect in the official decision-making process rested with the fact that no such group exclusion of Italians or Germans from the Atlantic Coast was contemplated despite the disloyal activities of some persons of German and Italian stock there.[23] Justice Murphy therefore dissented "from this legalization of racism. Racial discrimination in any form and in any degree has no justifiable part whatever in our democratic way of life. It is unattractive in any setting, but it is utterly revolting among a free people who have embraced the principles set forth in the Constitution of the United States."[24]

In sum, the Court may choose to interpret the due process clause of the fifth amendment as protecting all persons from such caste-based defects in the national lawmaking process. This applies to *any* congressional action otherwise within its enumerated powers, including those designed to override the Court's interpretation of what constitutes national privileges or immunities as against the states under section 1 of the fourteenth amendment.

A Clear Statement Rule

The Court has chosen to use a clear statement rule in a variety of contexts in order to make sure that Congress clearly states, and that Congress thereby lets the people know, when and how decisions affecting important constitutional interests are at stake. In these cases, the Court requires that Congress itself make clear what issue is being resolved and that Congress itself has decided the issue on the merits. For example, rather than reach important constitutional questions, the Court has overturned the actions of federal executive officials and administrative agencies as beyond the scope of the congressional grant of authority.[25] In these cases, the Court strikes down the federal action on statutory grounds to avoid deciding the constitutional issue, often in seeming contradiction of its otherwise generous review of broad delegations by Congress to administrative agencies. This also serves as a signal to Congress and the American people that an important policy issue is at stake that must be considered carefully on the merits if Congress wishes to proceed with the substantive policy adopted by the federal agency or bureaucrat.[26]

To understand how this technique might be used, consider a congressional law that created local abortion boards in response to the Court's decision declaring that, within the first three months of any pregnancy, women have a privilege or immunity under section 1 of the fourteenth amendment as against any state regulation to make their own choice on whether to bear or beget a child. In this statute, Congress advises these local abortion boards to conduct hearings to determine whether the health of the mother is endangered by the pregnancy or childbirth and to weigh this risk against the life of the fetus, case-by-case. The statute gives the local abortion boards discretion either to order the woman to give birth to the child or to allow an abortion as it sees fit in weighing these two interests. In reviewing an appeal from a local abortion board's decision requiring a woman to bear a child against her will, the Court could overturn that ruling on the ground that Congress failed to give the abortion board adequate guidance and thereby wrongly attempted to avoid making the substantive policy choice by shifting decision on the merits of a critical national legislative choice to diverse local abortion boards.

Similarly, the Court has often chosen to interpret congressional legislation to avoid issues of constitutional import unless the Congress makes a clear statement that it intends to enact the policy choice that directly raises the issue. For example, in a wide variety of federalism cases related to the allocation of powers between the national government and the states, the Court requires a clear statement by the Congress if it intends federal legislation to override, preempt, or otherwise displace the discretion of the states. Thus, for example, the Court has required a clear indication from Congress if it chooses to exercise its commerce clause powers to preempt the states, its spending powers to dictate policy to the states, or any of its enumerated powers to bring the states to heel in federal courts.[27] As another example, the Court sometimes construes congressional legislation narrowly to avoid the appearance of conflict with a previous Supreme Court ruling, unless the Congress makes clear that it is directly challenging or otherwise seeking to override the Court's previous judgment.[28]

Consider, for example, an arguably ambiguous congressional response to the Court's judgment that a woman's choice of whether to bear or beget a child is protected under the privileges or immunities clause from state regulation. The congressional act provides only that the life of the fetus shall be preserved unless the mental or physical health of the woman may be impaired. In reviewing this statute, the Court could interpret the statute as intended to implement guidelines similar to those set down by the Court in its original judgment in weighing the mother's interest in her own well-being against the government's interest in the preservation of the life of the fetus. By so doing, the Court would essentially send the substantive policy choice back to Congress for a second look at the merits of the competing interests at stake.

Laurence Tribe argues that the clear statement rule provides an important political check on the process of congressional lawmaking in all of these cases: where the balance between the interests of the national government, the states, and the individual are at stake, Congress "must be prevented from resorting to ambiguity as a cloak for its failure to accommodate the competing interests. . . ."[29] Perhaps, cases involving congressional legislation impacting those national privileges or immunities that the Court has held the states must respect under section 1 of the fourteenth amendment may be the most appropriate for application by the

Court of such a clear statement rule. When such critical individual rights, state interests, and substantive national policies are at stake, the people are entitled to know what it is that their representatives in Congress are deciding. The Court may use such techniques of construction to make sure that the people's representatives in Congress do not abuse the national lawmaking process by making decisions on such critical issues without airing the conflicting claims or actually resolving the issues on the merits in a visible fashion.[30]

Conclusion

Together, representation-reinforcing values, the anticaste principle, and the clear statement rule offer the Court an opportunity to shape but *not* ultimately to dictate the outcome of the process by which we the people engage in a dialogue through our elected representatives in Congress over what substantive national rights and regulations should control our conduct. As such, these three techniques represent choices for judicial review of the national lawmaking process which the Court may select if it wishes to embrace provisional review. They represent limits on the structure of the process of national lawmaking, not restrictions on the substantive policies that Congress determines to enact into law.

There are, however, two remaining interpretive choices that the Court *must* make in order to complete the structure for provisional review. First, the Court must explicitly choose what this elaboration of provisional review has only assumed—to interpret the Constitution so that an act of Congress within its enumerated powers authorizes the states to take actions which a previous judicial ruling under the privileges or immunities clause of the fourteenth amendment prohibited.[31] As discussed in chapter 2, this seeming anomaly arises from the structure of the Constitution: the privileges or immunities clause limits the states, but Congress is not limited by the privileges or immunities clause.

The Court has not had to face this issue because it has chosen to read the due process clauses of the fifth and fourteenth amendments as the open-ended invitation to articulate substantive rights. The cost of that choice has been, of course, to make the Court both the initial declarer and the final arbiter in interpreting what substantive rights bind both the states and the federal government. That choice places the Court in direct conflict with majority rule in a representative democracy. In contrast, the choice to permit Congress to exercise its enumerated powers to establish national substantive policies which the states may thereafter follow allows the Court to initiate a national dialogue over such substantive rights consistent with majority rule in the national legislature in which all of the people are represented. Indeed, this choice *is* authorized by the structure of the Constitution and better fits the text and purposes of both due process clauses and of the privileges or immunities clause of the fourteenth amendment.

Second, the Court must refuse to interpret the ninth amendment as an invitation to declare open-ended rights, nowhere else articulated in the Constitution, as against the national government.[32] To date, the full Court has not based any decision overturning an act of Congress on the ninth amendment. Nevertheless, the language permits a reading that would allow the Court to strike down an act of Congress that denies "rights retained by the people."[33] Indeed, for those who would prefer that the Court act as the final arbiter on substantive rights with respect to Congress as well, the ninth amendment surely provides in its text and relationship to the entire structure of the Constitution a better vehicle than the due process clause of the fifth amendment.

But this reading of the ninth amendment as an open-ended substantive rights restriction on Congress is not required. The ninth amendment can also be read as a declaration that the enumeration of rights elsewhere in the Constitution is not intended to deprive any person of rights *otherwise* provided under state law.[34] Once again, principles of representative democracy counsel that the Court choose this interpretation in order to avoid being the final arbiter with respect to Congress as to what substantive rights a member of the national community should have beyond those enumerated elsewhere in the Constitution. At the very least, the Court should be very chary in playing this ultimate wild card to trump any act of Congress.

With these two choices understood and made, the structure of provisional review is complete. Provisional review allows the Court to articulate substantive rights against the states under the privileges or immunities clause of the fourteenth amendment, while leaving Congress generally free to enact national legislation establishing a different policy under its powers enumerated in article I. Through this process of judicial review and national legislation, the Court is able to initiate a dialogue with the people over the substantive meaning of the Constitution. At the same time, the Court retains the authority to assure that the national lawmaking process is in fact representative, free from caste-based defects, and visibly focused on the merits of these critical issues.*

*Under the Bill of Rights, these restrictions on the congressional lawmaking process have a corollary for individual rights: *procedural* protections for the individual when the federal government chooses to exercise its coercive powers against particular persons in criminal or civil actions. The warrant, indictment, and jury trial requirements of the fourth, fifth, and sixth amendments, the prohibitions against double jeopardy and compulsory self-incrimination in the fifth amendment, and the right to counsel in the sixth amendment are examples. To the full extent that the Court chooses to interpret these procedural restrictions as binding, Congress may *not* overturn Court rulings interpreting the due process clause of the fourteenth

NOTES

1. These restrictions are imposed on all national legislation, whether enacted in response to a national-state dispute resolved in the first instance by the Court or in response to a perceived national need unrelated to any federalism conflict. Consider, for example, the first amendment's prohibition against any national law abridging freedom of speech or the fourth amendment's protection against unreasonable searches of a person's papers. These can be interpreted by the Court as forbidding national laws passed pursuant to Congress's power under section 8 of article I "to establish post offices" that seek to exclude political advertising from the U.S. mails or which require U.S. postal officials to search without any reason every person's mail for such political matter. The same sorts of constraints can also be read as applying to congressional attempts to substitute its judgment for that of the Court in resolving disputes between claimed national rights under section 1 of the fourteenth amendment and state interests. For example, if the Court declared that state laws forbidding criticism of a governor or requiring the search of every person's home for political materials "abridge the privileges of immunities of citizens of the United States," congressional acts seeking to authorize such unreasonable searches and restrictions on free speech could also be ruled unconstitutional under the first and fourth amendments. *See, generally,* L. TRIBE, AMERICAN CONSTITUTIONAL LAW 297, 326–27 (1988).
2. This is particularly true if the Court chooses to interpret the fifth amendment's prohibition against depriving any person of life, liberty, or property, without due process of law, as only a procedural limit. As discussed in chapter 1, the similarly worded due process clause of section 1 of the fourteenth amendment may have had a substantive connotation in the 1860s in the minds of some; and, by the turn of the century, the Court had chosen to give a substantive reading to the due process clause as the *Lochner* era unfolded. For the reasons detailed in chapters 1 and 2, however, the structure and text of section 1 both suggest that the Court could choose to interpret the fourteenth amendment's due process clause for what it says—a procedural restraint—and leave substantive rights restrictions on state power for interpretation under the privi-

amendment as providing such procedural protections when a person is confronted by the state in criminal or civil actions. In these areas, as in judicial review of the process of congressional lawmaking, the Court's rulings do *not* finally determine the ultimate substantive value choices. The Court assures, for example, only a fair trial to the person accused of any particular crime, not a verdict of not guilty. As with judicial review of the process of congressional lawmaking (and the refereeing of separation of power disputes), the Court does *not* evaluate the merits of the substantive policy choice made by the legislature, here outlawing certain conduct. Such value choices are therefore ultimately left for decision by the people's elected representatives rather than by the Court.

leges or immunities clause. With respect to the framing of the fifth amendment, there may be even less historical and textual warrant for choosing to give due process a substantive meaning. *See, e.g.,* J. ELY, DEMOCRACY AND DISTRUST 15 (1980). And the Court's only foray prior to the adoption of the fourteenth amendment into reading the fifth amendment's due process clause substantively—in the *Dred Scott* case—was a disaster. In sum, the Constitution authorizes the Court to choose to interpret the due process clause of the fifth amendment as imposing only fair process constraints on the national lawmaking power. Although this choice is not compelled, it would promote provisional review by enabling the people, through their representatives in Congress, to respond through ordinary national legislation to the Court's interpretation of most national substantive rights under the privileges or immunities clause of the fourteenth amendment.

3. *See* J. ELY, DEMOCRACY AND DISTRUST (1980).
4. *See, supra,* chapter 1, text at and notes 76–77; and Dimond, *The Anti-Caste Principle,* 30 WAYNE L. REV. 1 (1983).
5. *See, e.g.,* L. TRIBE, AMERICAN CONSTITUTIONAL LAW 890–904, 1314–29 (1988); Chaffee, Book Review in 62 HARV. L. REV. 891 (1949).
6. *See, e.g.,* J. ELY, *supra* note 3, at 105–16; A. MEIKLEJOHN, POLITICAL FREEDOM (1960); L. TRIBE, *supra* note 5, at 785–1024; Bork, *Neutral Principles and Some First Amendment Problems,* 47 IND. L.J. 1 (1971): Blasi, *The Checking Value in First Amendment Theory,* 1977 AMER. BAR FDTN. RES. J. 521.
7. J. ELY, *supra* note 3, at 106.
8. *See* L. TRIBE, *supra* note 5, at 785–94, 977–86. *Also, e.g.,* Police Department of the City of Chicago v. Mosley, 408 U.S. 92, 95–96 (1972); Schneider v. State, 308 U.S. 147 (1939); Kovacs v. Cooper, 336 U.S. 77 (1949); Keyishian v. Board of Regents, 385 U.S. 589 (1967).
9. Similarly, the prohibitions against bills of attainder and ex post facto laws in section 9 of article I and the limitations on the crime of treason against the United States in section 3 of article III may be read, in part, as also restricting the ability of the elected "ins" of the moment to stick it to political opponents who are out.
10. The seventeenth amendment, adopted in 1913, substituted direct election of senators by the people for the election of senators by the legislatures of each state originally provided by section 3 of article I.
11. 376 U.S. 1, 7–8 (1964).
12. Although the text of the Constitution permits this interpretation, it is not compelled by the language, the history of the framing of article I, or even the subsequent framing of the various amendments expanding the franchise, first to blacks, then to women, then to persons too poor to pay a poll tax, and finally to eighteen-year-olds. Curiously, John Ely in his elaboration of representation-reinforcing review does not discuss Justice Black's interpretation of section 2 of article I, nor the apportionment of the House of Representatives at all. He appears to limit his support of the "one person, one vote" standard to a combination of interpretations of the equal protection clause of the fourteenth amendment and of the

guarantee to every state in section 4 of article IV of a "republican form of government." J. ELY, DEMOCRACY AND DISTRUST 121–25 (1980). By their own terms, however, these two protections of representative democracy read as if to apply only to the states and not to Congress.

13. Consider, for example, a situation in which House districts were malapportioned for decades so that one-sixth of the voters controlled a majority of the seats and that the minority interests supporting this "majority" continued to control the political process by which decisions on any future apportionments would be made. Is such a systematically *unrepresentative* legislature representative in any democratic sense? Surely, the minority of one-sixth who are in control of the process of government are not to be trusted to give up their control of the legislature to the five-sixths who they have systematically fenced out of all opportunity to meaningfully influence the political process. J. ELY, DEMOCRACY AND DISTRUST 124 (1980). Indeed, the hegemony vested in the one-sixth over the five-sixths smacks of a "we-they" type discrimination which ought not be allowed to infect the process of electing representatives to the legislature in a representative democracy. *See also* Rogers v. Lodge, 458 U.S. 613 (1982) (discrimination against blacks in districting scheme); Harper v. Virginia Bd. of Elections, 383 U.S. 663 (1966) (poll tax); Kramer v. Union Free School District, 395 U.S. 621 (1969) (ownership of taxable property as qualification to vote).
14. *Compare* Bolling v. Sharp, 347 U.S. 497 (1954), *with* J. ELY, *supra* note 3, at 33–34.
15. Bolling v. Sharp, 347 U.S. at 499.
16. J. ELY, *supra* note 3, at 137.
17. 413 U.S. 528, 534 (1973).
18. 347 U.S. at 499.
19. *See* chapter 1 *supra*, text at notes 26–30; Dimond, *The Anti-Caste Principle*, 30 WAYNE L. REV. 1, 25 (1983).
20. *See* chapter 1 *supra*, text at note 88; Dimond, *Provisional Review*, HASTINGS CONST. L.Q. 201, 226 n.101 (1985).
21. *See* chapter 1 *supra*, text at notes 76–79.
22. The text and structure of the Constitution may be read to provide a different form of protection against caste discrimination under the due process clause of the fifth amendment for federal actions from that for state action under the equal protection clause of the fourteenth amendment. As chapter 1, text at notes 80–84, demonstrates, section 1 may be read much more affirmatively as requiring the states to *afford* equal protection. For example, state refusals to protect against customs of caste (as in the Klan regime of terror in 1871) and state failures to remedy the systemic effects of the most entrenched discrimination (as faced the Court in the long line of affirmative duty cases on remedy following *Brown II*) can be understood as violations of equal protection. This is hardly surprising as it is the states under our federal system that have the *primary* responsibility over the lives of people. The framing and text of the fourteenth amendment recognized just this structure: section 1 imposed the duty to afford equal protection on the states in the first instance, while section 5 gave Congress the power but not

the duty to enforce the people's rights under section 1 upon any state default. In contrast, national lawmaking is premised on enumerated powers and is largely interstitial in character. Only with respect to the lives of persons in the District of Columbia and U.S. territories has the Constitution vested the federal government with primary responsibility. As a result, any affirmative duty on the Congress to afford protection from caste may be limited to these federal enclaves. In other respects, the caste-based decisions of the Congress generally need only be invalidated by the Court as violations of due process of law under the fifth amendment and then remanded for another look without requiring any affirmative relief.

23. Justice Black in his opinion for the Court upholding this national action fell into a trap. Although conceding that the Japanese exclusion amounted to a "suspect" classification, he proceeded to argue that the special exigencies of war outweighed any right under the due process clause to be free from invidious discrimination in the official decisions of Congress and the executive in exercising their enumerated war powers. This attempt to weigh governmental necessity against the right to a process of decision making free from caste-based defects allowed Justice Black to conclude, in direct contradiction of the ugly facts, that "Korematsu was not excluded from the [West Coast] because of hostility to him or his race." This demonstrates why any "suspect classification" analysis must be understood and used only as a tool to ferret out whether such defects actually infected the decision-making process, rather than as an opportunity for the decision makers to justify actions tainted by such undue process. *See* J. ELY, DEMOCRACY AND DISTRUST 145–48 (1980); Dimond, *The Anti-Caste Principle*, 30 WAYNE L. REV. 1, 8 n.19 (1983); Dimond, *Provisional Review*, 12 HASTINGS CONST. L.Q. 201, 219 (1985). At the very least, if Justice Black had eschewed any such weighing of the governmental interest against the apparent racial discrimination, he might have inquired whether racial hostility to the Japanese played any part in the national decision-making process that led to the exclusion of only the Japanese from the West Coast, but not Germans from the East Coast. Surely, this type of inquiry would have led Justice Black to conclude that the "fit" between the stated goal of protecting the nation's coastal areas from invasion under the war powers enumerated in the Constitution and the means chosen of relocating only those of Japanese ancestry smacked of some caste-based taint in the decision-making process itself.
24. Korematsu v. United States, 323 U.S. 214, 235–42 (1944) (Murphy, J., dissenting).
25. *See, e.g.*, Hudson v. Goodwin, 11 U.S. (7 Cranch) 32 (1812) (free speech); Kent v. Dulles, 357 U.S. 116 (1958) (right to travel); Greene v. McElroy, 360 U.S. 474 (1959) (first amendment); New York Times v. United States, 403 U.S. 713 (1971) (free press); National Cable Television Ass'n v. United States, 415 U.S. 336 (1974) (extent to which Congress can delegate general taxing power to administrative agency); Hampton v. Mow Sun Wong, 426 U.S. 88 (1976) (foreign policy and

discrimination against aliens); and Pennhurst State School v. Halderman, 451 U.S. 1 (1981) (federal dictation to states of standards based upon spending power).

26. *See, generally,* J. Ely, *supra* note 3, at 131–34; L. Tribe, American Constitutional Law 365–66 (1988).
27. *See, e.g.,* Quern v. Jordan, 440 U.S. 332 (1979); Fitzpatrick v. Bitzer, 427 U.S. 445 (1976); Edelman v. Jordan, 415 U.S. 651 (1974); Employees v. Department of Public Health, 411 U.S. 279 (1973) (subjecting states to suits in federal courts in the face of the eleventh amendment); Pennhurst State School v. Halderman, 451 U.S. 1 (1981) (dictating standards to states under the spending power); and United States v. Bass, 404 U.S. 336 (1971) (displacing state regulation under the commerce power).
28. *See, e.g.,* Swann v. Charlotte-Mecklenberg Board of Education, 402 U.S. 1, 16–18 (1971) (antibusing legislation).
29. *See,* L. Tribe, American Constitutional Law 316–17 (1988). *Also, id.,* at 178–89, 323, 366.
30. There is also a constitutional basis for such remands by the Court to the legislature in order to require reconsideration of the merits of legislation. Some call this "means scrutiny," "rational relationship review with teeth," or "structural due process." *See* Gunther, *A Model for a Newer Equal Protection,* 86 Harv. L. Rev. 1 (1972); Weinberger v. Wiesenfeld, 420 U.S. 636, 650 (1975); Hampton v. Mow Sun Wong, 426 U.S. 88 (1976); Califano v. Goldfarb, 430 U.S. 199 (1977); United States Railroad Retirement Board v. Fritz, 449 U.S. 160, 186 (1980) (Brennan, J., dissenting); L. Tribe, American Constitutional Law 1677–87 (1988); Tribe, *Structural Due Process,* 10 Harv. Civ. Rts. Civ. Lib. L. Rev. 269, 314–18 (1976). The point of these approaches is to examine the *process* of lawmaking to make sure that the substantive decision has actually been made by Congress: unless the legislated means actually fit the goals articulated by the Congress, there may have been confusion about what was being legislated. This concern for the process of lawmaking is consistent with the object and operation of representation-reinforcing review, the anticaste principle, and the clear statement rule discussed in text above. These approaches are designed to make sure that Congress legislates in a visible fashion on the merits of issues. Upon finding a defect in the lawmaking process, the Court generally mandates what amounts only to a "suspensive veto" striking down the statute, rule, or regulation in question for the time being; this operates to remand the issue for reconsideration by the Congress but leaves Congress free to decide the remanded issue on the merits if it chooses to do so. *See* Sandalow, *Judicial Protection of Minorities,* 75 Mich. L. Rev. 1162, 1187–90 (1977); Dimond, *Provisional Review,* 12 Hastings Const. L.Q. 201, 221 (1985); L. Tribe, American Constitutional Law 1680–81 (1988). Although there are legitimate concerns as to the scope of this judicial oversight of the lawmaking process (*see* J. Ely, Democracy and Distrust 125–31 (1980)), cases that involve congressional attempts to substitute its judgment for that of the Court and

the states on what should constitute the national privileges or immunities of citizens are surely prime candidates.

31. *See* chapter 2 *supra,* text at notes 31–35.
32. The ninth amendment provides, "The enumeration in the Constitution, of certain rights, shall not be construed to deny or disparage others retained by the people."
33. *See* J. ELY, *supra* note 3, at 34–41.
34. *See* Dimond, *supra* note 20, at 227–28.

Part II

Provisional Review in Operation: Promoting a National Dialogue over the Meaning of the Constitution

CHAPTER 4 Freedom of Speech: Promoting Self-Expression while Protecting Political Discourse

Although Part I demonstrated in theory how the indeterminate nature and basic federal structure of the Constitution authorize provisional review, it is equally clear that the Court itself has never expressly embraced provisional review, except in a relatively narrow range of federalism cases. Part II therefore explores how provisional review might operate in practice if adopted by the Court in resolving a wide variety of human rights cases. For purposes of analysis, chapter 4 considers free speech, chapter 5 discrimination, chapter 6 abortion, and chapter 7 education. The range of examples is not exhaustive, but it does illustrate how provisional review might work to resolve a broader range of constitutional controversies.

Of necessity, the examples involve hypothetical fact situations, statutes, and governmental actions. As no Justice, let alone the entire Court, has based a personal rights opinion explicitly on the theory of provisional review, traditional legal analysis and criticism of prior judicial opinions are impossible. Part II therefore also uses hypothetical majority and minority opinions—and discussions in chambers among mythical Justices—to show how the tensions of provisional review might be resolved in the context of concrete cases and the widely divergent political and judicial philosophies evident on the Warren, Burger, and Rehnquist Courts. These hypothetical cases, opinions, and debates among the Justices are not meant to predict the future nor to rewrite the past. They are intended only to offer a lens through which to explore the potential for provisional review—and the resulting dialogue between the Court and the people over the meaning of the Constitution—if provisional review were adopted over time by the Court.

Each of the hypothetical cases begins with the Court positing a national right as against the states under section 1 of the fourteenth amendment. Each of the examples then explores how the Court might review the responses of Congress under provisional review. At the outset of this exploration, it is important to remember that none of the three types of structural limits that provisional review imposes on national legislation compels Congress to reach a particular substantive result. Representation-reinforcing values merely assure that the election of Congress and the political debate will be conducted consistent with a representative democracy so that the voices of all of the people can be meaningfully heard and counted. The anticaste principle prevents any group in power from acting out of prejudice to identify an out-group for relegation to a subordinate caste. The clear statement rule and related constitutional doctrines require only that the Congress actually articulate and decide for itself the merits of the issues over the meaning of the Constitution. In general, in reviewing these three limits on congressional lawmaking power, the Court does not tell the Congress what substantive outcome is finally required, only that the process of national lawmaking must be conducted in a fundamentally fair and open manner.

For the first hypothetical case concerning free speech, assume that a state passes a law permitting its courts to enjoin protests against the Governor when she is appearing in public, if the state court finds that such protests are likely to interfere with the ability of the Governor's audience to hear her speech. Assume that the Attorney General seeks an injunction in state court to prohibit a right-to-life demonstrator from appearing at the Governor's speech to a pro-choice rally on the steps of the Statehouse urging state funding of abortions as part of the Medicaid funding package for the poor.* Upon review, the case eventually reaches the United States Supreme Court, which decides that the state statute abridges the national privileges or immunities belonging to citizens under section 1 of the fourteenth amendment. In support of this conclusion, the Court reasons that the state statute is designed to regulate the content of speech in that it applies only to those who protest rather than support the Governor's positions. As such, the Court holds this statute a per se violation of what the Court has interpreted is a personal privilege or immunity to engage in political speech under section 1 of the fourteenth amendment free from state abridgement.

The President, himself a former Governor and the subject of similar protests that are disrupting his own public appearances, huddles with his leadership in Congress. Eventually, Congress enacts two laws within its enumerated powers. The first provides that the Attorney General of the United States may seek injunctions in federal courts against protests at public appearances of the President within the District of Columbia or any other federal territory, property, or enclave, whenever the Court finds a likelihood that the protest will interfere with the ability of others in the audience to hear the President; the second authorizes the states to pass similar legislation with respect to protests at public appearances of their own Governors on state grounds.[1]

*Or the hypothetical could be posed in the converse, with a right-to-life Governor appearing on the steps of the Statehouse to protest state funding, over the Governor's veto, of abortions for the poor, with the Attorney General seeking an injunction against a pro-choice demonstrator.

In appropriate cases or controversies, both laws eventually return to the Supreme Court for review as a result of court injunctions issued to prevent, for example, protests at the President's second inaugural address on the steps of the Capitol and the Governor's inaugural address in front of the Statehouse. As to the first, the Court must first review the act pursuant to representation-reinforcing review under the first amendment. Has Congress made a law "abridging the freedom of speech . . . or the right of the people peaceably to assemble, and to petition the Government for a redress of grievances"? In interpreting the first amendment, the Court no doubt could hold that the act amounts to just such an unconstitutional law: the act can be seen as a per se violation of the first amendment because Congress sought to regulate the content of speech.[2]

As to the second injunction, the state defense is not premised on any power of Congress to tell the Court how to interpret the meaning of the privileges or immunities clause of the fourteenth amendment. Instead, the state claims that its action is authorized by a national law, passed within the enumerated powers of Congress; as such, it represents just another example of the Congress resolving disputes between the national interest and state power. Although the Court agrees with the structure of the state's argument, it proceeds to review whether the congressional act itself, which authorized the state action, violates the first amendment. On this score, there can be no doubt that the congressional authorization is also a per se violation of the first amendment because the act authorizing the states to enjoin protests at the public appearances of their Governors is also aimed at the content of speech.

Following these Supreme Court rulings, does Congress (or the states) have any leeway in reenacting similar legislation? The Court's interpretation of the meaning of free speech under the first amendment and of the national privileges or immunities under section 1 of the fourteenth amendment permits *no* law regulating the content of political speech. Note, however, that such representation-reinforcing review says nothing about the merits of whether or not Congress or the states must, may, should, or should not fund abortions for the poor. Moreover, if the Congress or the states choose not to regulate the content of the speech but instead seek to regulate evenhandedly the time, place, or manner of demonstrations, whether in support or in opposition of elected officials, different issues may arise for decision by the Court.[3] Insofar as such regulation abridges political speech, however, the first amendment should be read by a provisional review Court as providing as tough a standard for protecting freedom of speech from congressional abridgment as is the privileges or immunities clause from state abridgment. With respect to political expression, there is not likely to be much play in the joints for different readings so long as the Court determines that the privileges or immunities clause protects political speech. If the Court chooses to interpret section 1 of the fourteenth amendment as guaranteeing freedom of political expression from state abridgment, it should come as no surprise that the Court chooses to read the more direct text of the first amendment as prohibiting any congressional attempt to abridge freedom of such speech.[4]

A different result is possible with respect to speech or expression that is not political in nature. Consider, for example, a state law prohibiting entertainers from performing at public functions in public places where citizens gather to hear and respond to political ideas. At joint appearances of the pro-choice Governor and her pro-life opponent to debate the abortion issue, a juggler regularly attends and performs before and after the debate while the audience arrives and departs. At one of these debates at a municipal stadium, the local police ask the juggler to stop performing, and, when he refuses, they cite him for a violation of the statute and book him. At his trial for violating the statute, the juggler shows that he did not disrupt the gubernatorial debate in the slightest. When asked what he was trying to communicate with his act, the juggler responds, "I wasn't trying to make any political statement of any kind. It makes me feel good to juggle and to watch and listen as the audience responds with clapping, laughter, and, when my act is really on a roll, cries of amazement."[5]

Eventually, this case reaches the United States Supreme Court to review the conviction and $100 fine imposed on the juggler for violating the state statute. The Court determines that, although the juggling at issue does not involve any political speech, there is also a national privilege or immunity protecting freedom of nonpolitical expression that the states must respect. In attempting to draw guidelines for the limits of this national right against the states, however, the Court expresses some reluctance and puzzlement. All that the Court is willing to say is that the facts of this particular case show that the state unduly burdened the entertainer's means of expression when the entertainer is willing to abide by any reasonable restrictions to assure the free flow of others' political ideas without any disruption in public forums. The Court, however, goes out of its way to explain how important the flow of artistic, literary, and scientific expression has been and will continue to be for the growth, diversity, and well-being of the nation.

At its next session, Congress considers the Court's juggling decision. Although there is agreement by many elected representatives with the Court's basic goal of freedom of nonpolitical expression, others are troubled by the Court's apparent attempt to strip the states of their discretion to balance other interests against this goal and then to strike a balance for themselves. Unable to resolve the issues for itself, Congress compromises and passes an act, in the words of its preamble, "to implement the freedom of nonpolitical expression announced by the Supreme Court" in the juggler's case. The Act creates a federal agency to promulgate regulations to guide the states in coming up with their own balance between freedom of nonpolitical expression and other interests. The agency proceeds to promulgate a number of regulations, including one that allows states to prohibit any entertainment at the public appearances of any political candidate, unless agreed to by the political candidate and the agency that controls the particular public forum. Pursuant to that regulation, the state passes such a statute, the local agency in charge of a public forum forbids entertainment of any kind at the next gubernatorial debate, the juggler appears and once again is charged, convicted, and fined $100 for violating the state law.

Once again, the case comes before the Supreme Court for review. The state defends the statute on the ground that it has been passed pursuant to a congressional statute within the enumerated powers of Congress, not that Congress or the agency is telling the Court how to interpret the privileges or immunities clause of the fourteenth amendment. As a result, the state argues, the Court's review should focus on the constitutionality of the congressional act and the federal agency's implementing regulations. Although the Court agrees with the structure of the state's argument, several important issues remain. First, should the first amendment prohibition against Congress making any law abridging freedom of speech be interpreted to cover nonpolitical as well as political expression? Second, should Congress in the guise of enacting a statute to implement freedom of nonpolitical expression be allowed to delegate decision on the actual policies to a federal agency without any adequate guidelines? Third, is the regulation promulgated by the federal agency that restricts freedom of nonpolitical expression consistent with the articulated purpose of the congressional statute?

Rather than reach the constitutional issue of the meaning of the free speech clause of the first amendment for nonpolitical expression, the Court strikes down the state criminal conviction on two alternative grounds. First, although broad discretion is usually granted to Congress in establishing the operation of federal agencies, Congress in the "Freedom of Nonpolitical Expression Act" failed to give adequate policy guidance to the agency. Second, the articulated purpose of the statute, to promote freedom of nonpolitical expression, does not fit the anti-entertainment regulation promulgated by the agency. The Court's opinion concludes, "Where important national rights of individuals and the meaning of the Constitution are at stake, we hold that Congress must decide the issues for decision on the merits by a clear statement, not by misleading the American public by passing a statute that claims to do one thing, but then delegates responsibility for establishing policy to a federal agency that proceeds to do exactly the opposite."

In response to this ruling, one can imagine the Congress simply allowing the Freedom of Nonpolitical Expression Act and its agency to expire. At the very least, if Congress chooses to consider the issue again, the people will be able to know what it is that their representatives are deciding and will be free to lobby them on the merits of the issue. For purposes of analysis, however, assume that Congress after much debate responds by passing a "Regulation of Nonpolitical Expression Act." In this statute, Congress makes clear its policy that nonpolitical expression may be regulated as to time, place, and manner and may be prohibited altogether by the states, if they wish, at any public forum in which political ideas are being discussed. To emphasize this point, Congress also passes a statute making it a crime for any person to engage in nonpolitical expression at any public forum on federal land when political ideas are being expressed. Once again, the state passes its anti-entertainment statute, the juggler is convicted for violating the state statute at the next gubernatorial debate and, for good measure, the juggler is also convicted for violating the federal statute for juggling at the next presidential inauguration in front of the steps of the Capitol.

On review of these convictions, the Supreme Court is now squarely faced with the issue of the meaning of the first amendment with respect to nonpolitical expression. Under *Marbury*, the Court has the responsibility for interpreting the meaning of the first amendment. If the Court chooses to hold that the first amendment protects nonpolitical expression as vigorously as political expression, the people will be able to respond to this decision only by a process of evolution, new appointments to the Court, or constitutional amendment. From the perspective of provisional review, however, it is also possible that the Court will defer to Congress in this case, at least so long as the Court is certain that no particular harmful message or remotely political idea is being attacked.

Unless the Court determines that there is some risk that Congress or the state is really attempting to regulate entertainment generally or juggling in particular as some kind of potentially dangerous message, why should the Court choose to interpret the first amendment as disabling Congress from regulating nonpolitical expression? Nonpolitical expression may not even be much endangered if freedom of speech in the first amendment is read under provisional review as protecting primarily political expression essential for the functioning of a representative democracy.* In any event, we the people can be assured that we will be able to

*Indeed, provisional review provides the Court with the opportunity to interpret the right of nonpolitical expression broadly under the privileges or immunities clause of the fourteenth amendment against state abridgment in the first instance. As a result, the Court will have the opportunity to persuade the people, and their elected representatives in Congress, of the importance of such nonpolitical expression. Depending on how the Court chooses to use this opportunity and the people respond over time in the dialogue with the Court, provisional review very well could end up with *more* protection of nonpolitical, as well as political, expression. Any rule that requires the Court to provide exactly the same protection of all expression under the first amendment against the federal government as the Court provides under section 1 of the fourteenth amendment against state action might lead to *less* protection, even of political speech. *See, e.g.,* Debs v. United States, 249 U.S. 211 (1919) (upholding federal conviction of a socialist party presidential candidate convicted for an antiwar speech urging resistance to the draft); Walker v. Birmingham, 388 U.S. 307 (1967) (upholding Martin Luther King's conviction for leading a civil rights march in violation of state court's *ex parte* injunction against the march).

continue to debate the issue of the importance of nonpolitical expression and choose to elect representatives in Congress, the statehouses, and city halls who will promote nonpolitical expression and weigh any competing interests with sensitivity.

Viewed from this perspective, the Court under provisional review may be seen as playing three critical roles. First, in interpreting the privileges or immunities clause broadly as protecting nonpolitical expression from state abridgment, the Court stimulates national discussion of the issue. Second, by assuring that Congress decides such issues on the merits, rather than hiding a contrary decision behind affirmative language or passing the buck on the decision to unelected agencies without any policy guidance, the people will be able to know what their representatives are deciding so that these elected officials can be influenced prior to voting on the merits and thereafter held accountable for their vote. Third, in strictly enforcing the first amendment protection of freedom of political speech from congressional abridgment, the Court can assure that we the people will always be able to debate openly the issue of the extent to which nonpolitical speech should be promoted and protected; and that no government, in the guise of regulating nonpolitical expression, is able to abridge any particular message because the government deems its content dangerous.

This approach will encourage the people and their elected representatives to reflect upon the wisdom, costs, and benefits of regulating various types of nonpolitical expression in diverse contexts. Ultimately, however, the Court's word on nonpolitical expression need not be final for provisional review, and representative democracy, to work.

NOTES

1. Note that neither act attempts to tell the Court directly that it must interpret the privileges or immunities or free speech clauses in a particular fashion. This is because the Congress does not want to run afoul of the *Marbury* doctrine that it is the Court's duty to interpret the meaning of the Constitution. *See, e.g.,* United States v. Klein, 80 U.S. (13 Wall.) 128, 146–47 (1872).
2. *See* discussion *supra,* Chapter 3, text at notes 6–8.
3. The first issue would be whether such a law, neutral on its face, was passed with the purpose of continuing to silence those who oppose the positions of elected officials. If such a purpose exists, the political "ins" are merely trying to choke off the "outs" from influencing the body politic. Assuming that the law was not passed to regulate the content of speech, serious first amendment issues concerning whether the law nevertheless impermissibly clogs up the channels of political communication would remain. Even if a law does not seek to silence a particular point of view, it may so effectively close off avenues for public debate as to threaten the open communication essential for the operation of a representative democracy.

See, e.g., J. ELY, DEMOCRACY AND DISTRUST 115–16 (1980); L. TRIBE, AMERICAN CONSTITUTIONAL LAW 789–94, 977–1010 (1988).

4. Under provisional review, this is an example of how the debate on whether the fourteenth amendment "incorporates" the Bill of Rights is rendered largely irrelevant. As we have seen in chapter 2, the sources for judicial interpretation of the privileges or immunities clause of the fourteenth amendment that binds the states are wide-ranging and may include, but are not limited to, the rights that the Bill of Rights requires the national government to respect. The more interesting question for provisional review is the extent to which the Bill of Rights can or should be interpreted to include as restrictions on the federal government the personal rights and duties which the Court interprets section 1 of the fourteenth amendment as imposing on the states.
5. The hypothetical example could be changed to cover other artistic, literary, or scientific expression, gatherings in a public forum, or commercial speech, which arguably do not involve political speech. *See, e.g.*, Meyer v. Nebraska, 262 U.S. 390 (1923) (teaching in German language at a private school); Virginia State Board of Pharmacy v. Virginia Consumer Council, 425 U.S. 748 (1976) (licensed pharmacist advertising prices of prescription drugs); and Coates v. City of Cincinnati, 402 U.S. 611, 615 (1971) (gatherings on public sidewalks). The line between political and nonpolitical expression is, of course, hardly precise. *Cf.* L. TRIBE, AMERICAN CONSTITUTIONAL LAW 890–904 (1988) (criticizing the Court's attempts to distinguish commercial and noncommercial speech); L. BOLLINGER, THE TOLERANT SOCIETY (arguing for broad protection of all types of expressive speech and behavior as promoting political tolerance).

   Or the hypothetical example could be altered to cover self-expression, self-gratification or family autonomy, even in a somewhat less public setting, such as "shuffling Sam's" solo dance to a jukebox while waiting for a bus (Thompson v. Louisville, 362 U.S. 199 (1960)); a person's stroll on public streets in the evening (Kolender v. Lawson 461 U.S. 352 (1982)); viewing pornographic materials in the privacy of one's home (Stanley v. Georgia, 394 U.S. 557 (1964)); a family's choice to attend a private school (Pierce v. Society of Sisters, 268 U.S. 510 (1925)); or arrangements to live in an extended family within a community zoned for single, traditional nuclear families (Moore v. East City of East Cleveland, 431 U.S. 494 (1977)). Such self-actualization cases overlap the personhood issues discussed in chapter 6.

CHAPTER 5 Caste Discrimination: Prohibiting Caste-based Legislation while Promoting a Dialogue over Remedy

Reviewing Congressional Legislation for Discrimination

To understand the operation of provisional review in race cases, we must first consider how the Court could review congressional lawmaking for caste discrimination. Consider the following hypothetical. Imagine that Congress had responded to the Court's decisions in *Brown* and *Bolling* holding forced segregation in the public schools in the states and the District of Columbia unconstitutional in 1954 by passing the "Equal Educational Opportunity Act of 1957." In the preamble to this Act, Congress finds, "All Americans, regardless of race, should have the right to equal educational opportunities in public schools, both in the states and in the District of Columbia." Based on the evidence obtained at extensive congressional hearings, the preamble to the Act continues,

> The Congress agrees with the United States Supreme Court's recent rulings requiring that equal educational opportunities be made available to all children regardless of race. We also agree that separate educational facilities are inherently unequal insofar as they are premised on the white supremacy myth that black children are so inferior that they should not be allowed to attend school with white children. But the preponderance of the evidence demonstrates that black and white children will both be able to attain their right to equal educational opportunities better if taught in separate schools through age sixteen by teachers of their own race with classmates of their own race. The Congress also specifically finds that this is a matter solely of educational policy and specifically rejects any connotation that such separate schooling implies the inferiority of blacks compared to whites or any other race. Our goal is to assist all of the people of this nation, the states, and the District of Columbia to comply with the Supreme Court's interpretation of the fifth and fourteenth amendments in *Brown* and *Bolling*.

To implement this policy, the Act directs the states and the District of Columbia to provide separate schools of comparable quality in all material respects to all children through age sixteen and the right of all qualified children seventeen or older to seek further schooling in high schools, colleges, and graduate schools in the school of each child's choice, subject only to reasonable regulations unrelated to the race of the child.

The legislative history reflects that the 1957 Equal Educational Opportunity Act is a compromise hammered out by moderates in response (*a*) to the calls of many in states with mandatory segregation laws for massive resistance to the Court's decrees[1] and (*b*) the calls of others in states with either few blacks or blacks concentrated in a few heavily black school districts for immediate desegregation of the public schools. Although there were then only a few black representatives in the House and none in the Senate, many blacks did testify at congressional hearings on the proposal. Some black educators and self-styled radicals testified to the potential benefits of preparing blacks in separate schools in order to unite for the struggle to survive in what remained basically a segregated society still premised on the myth of white supremacy. At the same time they warned of the damage that would befall black children from trying to learn in formerly white schools with white teachers, administrators, and students openly hostile to the black students.[2] Other black educators and political leaders conceded that the quality of education was important to all children. But they wanted segregated systems of schooling completely dismantled, not because black schools or teachers were inferior to white schools or teachers, but because "we want to do away with a system that exalts one class and debases another."[3]

Contemporaneously, Congress passes the "Public Safety and Order Act of 1957," which provides in pertinent part that all previously segregated "public swimming pools, beaches, parks, drinking fountains, and golf courses shall be closed until the President finds that they can be reopened safely without threat of disorder; and all public transportation systems, hospitals, and rest rooms shall be operated on a segregated basis until the President finds that the threat of imminent racial disorder has subsided."

The preamble to this Act notes,

> Congress finds a national emergency has arisen because of the Supreme Court's recent rulings applying *Brown* to other public facilities without even offering an opinion as to why the "separate but equal" doctrine no longer has any place in public services other than education. The Congress finds that the rationale given by the Court in *Brown,* to provide an equal educational opportunity to all children, has no relevance to other public facilities. As a result of the confusion over the meaning of these Supreme Court rulings without opinions, both blacks and whites now find themselves

> thrown together in hostile mobs in public facilities, which are rapidly becoming unusuable by any person, white or black. Until this crisis of public order subsides, Congress finds that nonessential public services should be closed altogether and essential services operated on a segregated basis, both in the states and in the District of Columbia. We take this extraordinary action not to challenge the Court's authority to issue the judgments in question, but to allow the Court the opportunity to consider the possibility of error and, in any event, to delay implementation until the national crisis of violent disorder subsides.

The legislative history reveals that this Act is also the product of a compromise hammered out by moderates in Congress between (*a*) those who urge massive resistance to the *per curiam* decisions of the Supreme Court outlawing forced segregation in all such public facilities and (*b*) those in states with few blacks or with blacks concentrated in a few municipalities who urge immediate desegregation of all public facilities. With a few notable exceptions,[4] all segments of the black leadership testify that it is the responsibility of the Congress and the President, if they are going to do anything at all, to put the full weight of the national government behind ending mandatory segregation of such public facilities rather than catering to the white mobs in some places who are attacking blacks who attempt to make use of the whites-only beaches, golf courses, pools, drinking fountains, rest rooms, buses, and hospitals.

In tandem, these two acts offer a haunting refrain from the racial dilemma that faced the nation in the decades immediately after the Civil War. Once again, the dominant white majority, but this time in the form of national legislation rather than state laws, seeks to rationalize the forced segregation of blacks from whites. Once again, there are understandable strains within the black community over how to overcome the caste system,[5] disagreements the white majority is quite happy to exploit. Once again, there is a claim by a dominant national voice, this time Congress rather than the *Plessy* Court, that segregation imposes no badge of inferiority on blacks.[6] Once again, there is the threat of racial violence if blacks choose to exercise their rights. Unlike the Ku Klux Klan Act of 1871, the Congress, rather than passing legislation to require the states to use their law-enforcement machinery to protect blacks from hostile white mobs, opts to keep blacks segregated from whites, even to the extent of closing all but the most essential public services ordinarily available in most states. Once again, the Court is faced with a decision that will impact the course of race relations in the country for decades to come. A constitutional crisis of the first order looms.

Eventually, the Supreme Court reviews each of these Acts in an appropriate case or controversy. Under the clear statement rule, the Court could overturn the Equal Educational Opportunity Act on the ground that

Congress has not clearly stated the issue for decision. The articulated premise of the Act is that educational opportunity as measured by the ability of the children to learn in segregated versus integrated schools provides the rationale for the Court's decisions in *Brown* and *Bolling*; the articulated goal of the statute is to assist in securing compliance with the Court's prior rulings. The Court in its opinion, therefore, could note how the Congress has failed to appreciate the anticaste underpinnings of the Court's segregation ruling:

> Although we indicated in *Brown* that "separate educational facilities are inherently unequal," we did not mean to imply that the measure of the constitutionality of governmentally mandated segregation was the quality of the education provided in separate as compared to unitary systems of public schooling. To the contrary, the whole point of our ruling was to recognize that state-mandated segregation is part and parcel of the Jim Crow caste system that sought to substitute segregation as the means to subordinate blacks to a second-class status after the Civil War Amendments and Reconstruction civil rights laws abolished slavery and the Black Codes. That is why we specifically overruled the language in *Plessy* that served both to rationalize and to promote segregation as the mechanism of caste for the next two generations. The suggestion that such a caste regime may be instantly transformed by a congressional claim that segregation in schools does not imply the inferiority of blacks sounds a haunting refrain to the similar rationalization in *Plessy* that we squarely rejected in *Brown*.

The Court's opinion continues,

> We assume, however, that Congress *is* serious in its stated purpose of assisting in securing full compliance with this Court's rulings in *Brown* and *Bolling*. Rather than reach the serious constitutional issues that might arise should Congress seek instead to overturn or to frustrate these decisions, we therefore hold that the 1957 Equal Educational Opportunity Act is invalid solely because its means of implementation are not rationally related to its stated purpose of enforcing this Court's rulings in *Brown* and *Bolling*. If our prior opinions contributed to the apparent confusion that led to this undue process of lawmaking, our clarification this day will assist the Congress, and the American people, to understand the critical nature of the constitutional interests at stake.

By thus spelling out the anticaste principle, the Court could thereby put Congress and the people of the nation on notice about the nature of this protection from any in-group seeking to relegate an out-group to a subordinate caste.[7]

The Court might also choose to use a clear statement approach to invalidate the Public Safety and Order Act:

> As noted in our ruling this day on the Equal Educational Opportunity Act, the Court's rulings in *Brown* and *Bolling* were premised on the unconstitutionality of any official caste system that seeks to relegate a person or group identified by the dominant majority to a subordinate status. Pursuant to normal practice in this Court, we limited our rulings in *Brown* and *Bolling* to the facts of the cases before us, namely the segregated systems of schooling mandated in some of the states and the District of Columbia. Thereafter, we applied the anticaste principle of these cases to strike down state-mandated segregation of all variety of public facilities and services. We did so through a series of one-sentence orders without opinion. We followed this practice because we did not want unnecessarily to arouse the hostility of the very local, state, and federal officials, who would have to carry out our decrees, by detailing their part in perpetuating the caste segregation at issue in each of those cases. Unfortunately, the premises articulated in the Public Safety and Order Act suggest that our use of *per curiam* opinions served to confuse the Congress and the American people on the nature of the wrong at issue in those cases.

The Court's opinion might then continue,

> If we were to review the merits of this Act, serious constitutional issues would arise as to whether the substantive provisions of the Act impermissibly seek to delegate to the executive the lawmaking powers specifically vested in Congress by section 8 of article I and by section 5 of the fourteenth amendment. If we were to review the merits of this Act, serious issues would also arise as to whether the Act's process of lawmaking has been influenced in violation of the due process clause of the fifth amendment by a racially discriminatory purpose of perpetuating a caste system. Indeed, it was only last year that each of the Justices signed the ruling in *Cooper v. Aaron* reminding state officials in Arkansas bent on perpetuating segregation in Little Rock's public schools that "the constitutional rights of [schoolchildren] are not to be sacrificed or yielded to the violence and disorder which have followed upon the actions of the Governor and the Legislature. . . . [L]aw and order are not here to be preserved by depriving the Negro children of their constitutional rights."[8] The President of the United States is to be commended

> for exercising the full range of his authorized powers to restrain the mob violence in Little Rock so that the plaintiff black schoolchildren would not be denied their constitutional rights by such obstruction.

The opinion might conclude,

> Now that we have clarified the unconstitutional nature of caste discrimination inhering in providing public services on a segregated basis, we anticipate that the Congress will be in a position to consider the merits of the issue whether violent objections by white mobs to the declared constitutional rights of our fellow black citizens in this country should be met by suspending constitutional rights or by controlling the mobs through the processes of law enforcement available at the local, state, and national level.

Even if the Congress in the passage of these two Acts was only attempting to feign misunderstanding of the Court's prior rulings in order to influence the Court to reconsider its position, the Court may respond under the clear statement rule by requiring that Congress instead take a second look at these two statutes. This would also serve the purpose of allowing the Court another opportunity to educate the people about the meaning of caste: this might serve to shame the Congress into rethinking its position rather than candidly admitting that it was attempting to frustrate the Court's rulings in *Brown* and *Bolling*.

Assume, however, that Congress responds by reenacting by a voice vote without debate the substantive provisions of both statutes without any preamble or making any findings. Under the anticaste principle of the due process clause of the fifth amendment, the Court would then have the duty to determine whether caste defects influenced the congressional lawmaking process or whether the congressional action otherwise sought to stamp blacks with a badge of inferiority.

The legislative history provides evidence that the decision-making process was influenced at least in part by a purpose to maintain the former caste system of segregation for as long as possible. First, the goals stated in the original versions of the Equal Educational Opportunity and Public Order Acts appear, at least in part, to be pretexts for continuing the system of caste segregation. Second, despite the availability of other means to achieve the stated goals (e.g., requiring the states to provide police protection and authorizing the use of federal troops as a backup to maintain order for all persons in the use and enjoyment of public services on a nonsegregated basis), the means chosen appear designed to maintain segregation in public facilities deemed essential and to close other public facilities threatened with nonsegregated use. Third, the timing of the reenactments with the same substantive provisions give little reason to believe that the caste influences that more clearly marked the initial versions played no part in the final legislation. Finally, given the historical context of forced segregation as a part of a regime of Jim Crow designed to relegate blacks to a second-class status, there can be little doubt that the Court should rule that this legislation violates the anticaste principle as much as the federal action compelling segregation of the District of Columbia schools originally ruled unconstitutional in *Bolling*.

From the perspective of provisional review, the anticaste principle counsels the Court to review the lawmaking of Congress with the same sensitive search for caste discrimination with which it should review state acts. Only then can all persons trust that the official decision-making process is not influenced by any majority's attempt to identify a minority and to relegate it to a subordinate position because of prejudice. Fortunately, the Congress and the President have not since *Brown* directly confronted the Court with legislation designed so to undermine the Court's anticaste interpretation of the fifth and fourteenth amendments; and the Court has been able to construe any potentially limiting legislation narrowly to avoid any direct confrontation.[9] But if such a battle is ever drawn, the Court has the responsibility under provisional review to examine thoroughly and to strike down finally any congressional lawmaking that has been tainted by any caste-based defect.

Under provisional review, it is important to remember that Congress is *not* barred from providing public order and safety in some public facilities and ordering that others be closed altogether. Nor is Congress prohibited from advancing the quality of public schools generally nor from promoting equal educational opportunity for children specifically. But Congress may not choose to do any such act when its decision-making process is influenced by prejudice against blacks, nor by selecting means that serve only to perpetuate the system of caste segregation. Although it may be difficult to apply an anticaste principle in reviewing the process of national lawmaking, it is an essential responsibility of the Court, particularly under provisional review. Congress should be given no more discretion under the due process of lawmaking guaranteed by the fifth amendment to impose caste than the states have under the equal protection clause of the fourteenth amendment.

Reviewing Remedial Legislation by Congress

If provisional review provides the Court with the means to scrutinize congressional legislation for forbidden caste discrimination, the question remains whether Congress is under any affirmative duty to remedy the constitutional violations described by the Court's rulings in *Bolling* and *Brown*. To answer this question, we need to look first at the structure of the Constitution and at the appropriate role of the courts in reviewing remedial proposals generally. With respect to the unconstitutional segregation of the District of Columbia schools, the answer might seem to be yes. With respect to this federal enclave, section 8 of article I gives Congress the "power . . . to exercise exclusive legislation . . . over such District (not exceeding ten miles square) as may . . . become the seat of government of the United States." Unless and until the Constitution is amended to make the District of Columbia a state with the primary responsibility of self-government over the lives of persons within that ten-mile square, *Bolling* and *Brown II* may be read as requiring the federal authority with ultimate responsibility over the District of Columbia "to effectuate a transition to a racially non-discriminatory school system."[10]

To avoid any direct constitutional confrontation with the Congress, however, the Court chose instead to direct its affirmative remedial decrees following *Brown* against the executive officials with responsibility over the administration of the public schools, both within the District of Columbia and within local school districts throughout the nation. Indeed, *Brown II* contemplated that any plan to remedy unconstitutional school segregation should be reviewed in the first instance by the trial court hearing the case. This procedure means that the flinty and more intractable considerations of remedy will be separated from the initial determination of the nature of any constitutional violation and the sweep of any resulting wrong.[11]

In addition to avoiding direct confrontations with the Congress (and the state legislatures), this bifurcation of right declaration in *Brown I* from hearing on remedy in *Brown II* provides the Court with the opportunity to maintain its *judicial* role throughout a case. At the remedy phase, courts may then continue to act as judicial bodies. The judiciary can review the remedial plans promulgated by the responsible executive officials through an adjudicative process, rather than falling prey to the temptation of formulating its own remedy plans. This is essential if courts are to maintain their independence and integrity. Courts need only *review* remedial proposals and any objections of the parties through the judicial process and make their judgments through judicial rulings. Courts do not need to become special masters or superintendents of operations of the public service at issue. Nothing can more surely erode the people's trust in the independent nature of the courts' voice than judges acting like self-anointed executive officials taking charge of a public service. Neither do judges have to act like negotiators meeting separately with the adverse parties to coerce a settlement with the threat of then donning the robes to exercise judicial power if the parties don't agree.[12]

Under this bifurcated approach to right declaration and remedial decrees, the courts may first review the remedial proposal to make sure that the executive officials' process of formulating the remedial plan is itself free from caste-based defects catering to the in-group's prejudice.[13] Second, the courts need only determine whether the proposed plan fits the wrong: the plan must actually address the *condition* that offends the Constitution. Beyond these two basic requirements, broad discretion may be vested in the responsible executive officials to work out the details, subject to the availability of the federal court to review the effectiveness of the remedial plan in operation.[14] For example, under this approach to judicial review of remedies, courts should strike down a plan that proposes to place the entire responsibility of desegregation on the black schoolchildren who were the primary victims of the violation, or a plan that seeks to pay black schoolchildren damages for the wrong of Jim Crow segregation as the price to keep the segregated system of schooling intact. Such plans are riven by caste and do not address the condition that offends the Constitution.[15]

Such a bifurcated approach to rights and remedies also gives Congress the opportunity to exercise its broader legislative powers to pass more comprehensive remedial legislation. To explore the potential extent of this congressional power, consider the following hypothetical: imagine that Congress investigated segregation in the District of Columbia following the Court's decisions in *Brown* and *Bolling* and found that the legacy of Jim Crow caste pervaded all aspects of housing, public services, employment opportunities, and community life throughout the entire metropolitan area, including the white suburbs in Virginia and Maryland. Under its plenary powers under the commerce clause and spending power, Congress could provide for a comprehensive program of majority-to-minority transfers between schools, a desegregative school construction program, ancillary relief to assist black children in competing fairly and encouraging white children to understand racial diversity, a variety of housing desegregation initiatives, affirmative employment measures, and desegregation programs for all public services and facilities throughout the metropolitan area of which the District of Columbia is a part. Under provisional review, the courts would review such an alternative proposal in light of the remedial standards set forth above. There is little doubt that the judiciary would *welcome* such a broad remedial program so long as it was not influenced by caste-based defects or otherwise served as a pretext for delay. Such an anticaste program surely would fit the caste wrong of systemic segregation.

That brings us to the issue of congressional power to remedy caste segregation within the states unrelated to the District of Columbia. Congress has no affirmative duty to eliminate unconstitutional school segregation outside federal enclaves. If Congress so chooses, it may just sit on the sidelines and watch as the federal courts review remedy plans proposed and implemented by state and local officials. Section 1 of the fourteenth amendment imposes the duty directly on the states to afford protection from the continuing effects of any caste system within their jurisdictions. The Congress does, however, have the power under section 5 of the fourteenth amendment and the powers enumerated in section 8 of article I to compel the states to meet their affirmative responsibility.

Consider, for example, how provisional review suggests the Court should review an affirmative congressional response to the Court's rulings in *Brown*. Imagine that Congress passes the "National Anticaste Act of 1964." In the preamble Congress recites,

> In hearing testimony on the Court's rulings in *Brown* and its progeny, we have come to understand that this nation is divided by a system of segregation in schools, housing, and all other aspects of community life, which has relegated blacks to a second-class status. When the Court belatedly challenged this system of caste as inconsistent with this nation's commitment to fundamental fairness in a representative democracy, Congress and the President did not perceive the national scope and pervasive reach of the problem of racial ghettoization in our metropolitan areas; nor did we always act steadfastly even in assuring that black citizens, who were only seeking to exercise their constitutional rights, were not subject to intimidation by mob violence. We therefore resolve this day to get on with the process of racial healing that will be necessary if our nation is to unite so that this one country will no longer be divided into two societies, one black, one white—separate and unequal.

In its substantive provisions, the Act calls for the states to submit comprehensive plans within one year to the President to provide on an area-wide basis for integrated educational opportunities to all schoolchildren, housing desegregation initiatives, community development plans, public and private employment opportunities, and multiracial observation teams. The Act authorizes the President, who had submitted the initial anticaste bill to Congress and worked for its passage, to approve any plan that actually addresses the area-wide systems of caste within the states and promises a substantial start on overcoming the caste system immediately. If the President finds the state plan inadequate, he is authorized to formulate his own plan for such defaulting states and to proceed to the federal district court to sue any defaulting state for appropriate enforcement orders. The Act provides for judicial review of the plans approved or formulated by the President, but requests the courts to permit implementation of the plans pending final judicial review. The Act provides for substantial federal funding to support plans approved or developed by the President; and the Act calls for the President to withhold all federal funds from any state that fails to submit a plan altogether, refuses to implement the plan approved or promulgated by the President, or refuses to obey any court order enforcing the Anticaste Act of 1964.

On review in an appropriate case, is there any doubt that a Court committed to provisional review would strive mightily to uphold this Act? The Court should hold that Congress has the power under section 5 of the fourteenth amendment and its plenary powers under section 8 of article I to pass the Act. Indeed, the Court might go out of its way to review the constitutionality of the Act on its face quickly in order to assure the American people that the Congress has the power to come to grips with the basic wrong and to direct the states to get on with the task of overcoming the system of caste segregation at issue in *Brown.*[16]

The Court would only inquire whether caste-based defects influenced the legislation and whether this remedial act addresses the basic wrong. The Court would breathe a sigh of relief, applaud Congress and the President, and stand ready to assist in reviewing appeals from the state plans as they arise to make sure that none of them is influenced by prejudice against any group that the states might seek to identify, or otherwise fail to address the area-wide systems of segregation found unlawful by Congress. Under provisional review, the Court should welcome the help of Congress in framing and implementing nondiscriminatory remedies that actually address the basic wrong at issue.

Provisional review, therefore, provides the Court with the means to encourage the people through their representatives in Congress to respond affirmatively with remedial proposals to overcome entrenched discrimination. At the same time, provisional review authorizes the Court to scrutinize the congressional lawmaking process to make sure that it directly addresses the merits of the wrong at issue without being influenced by any dominant majority in-group's desire to perpetuate any minority out-group in a subordinate caste. Provisional review provides the Court with the tools to distinguish between congressional attempts (*a*) to perpetuate mandatory segregation in schools and other public services under the pretext of promoting educational opportunity and public order and (*b*) to confront the wrong of segregation in all aspects of community life in America through a wide variety of innovative legislation. Through this judicial process the Court can promote an ongoing dialogue with the people over how to address caste discrimination that has already divided the country, while protecting against any new congressional legislation infected by caste discrimination.

NOTES

1. *See* "Southern Manifesto," 102 CONG. REC. 3984, 4004 (March 12, 1956) (signed by nineteen southern Senators and eighty-three southern Representatives). This resistance to the Court's rulings also took many other forms, ranging from white mob violence directed at blacks, which state and local law officers either ignored or promoted, to disingenuous schemes to close public schools altogether and to subsidize whites-only academies, to racially skewed pupil placement laws. *See, generally,* N. DORSEN, et al., POLITICAL AND CIVIL RIGHTS IN THE UNITED STATES 625–33 (1979).
2. *See, e.g.,* DuBois, *Does the Negro Need Separate Schools,* 4 J. NEG.

EDUC. 328, 335 (1935); Bell, *The Legacy of W.E.B. DuBois,* 11 CREIGHTON L. REV. 409, 419 (1977).

3. Quoting Frederick Douglass's plea for abolition of the color line in schooling during Reconstruction. M. WEINBERG, A CHANCE TO LEARN 51 (1977).
4. *Cf.* note 2 *supra*; and note 5 *infra*.
5. *Compare,* 3 BOOKER T. WASHINGTON PAPERS 584–86 (L. Harlan ed. 1974) (urging acceptance of segregation as the price for mutual economic progress of blacks and whites) *with* W.E.B. DUBOIS, THE SOULS OF BLACK FOLK 23, 48–49, 52–53 (1903. 1961 reprint) (urging blacks to challenge the color line and to protest any denial of political or civil rights). *See also,* Dimond & Sperling, *Of Cultural Determinism and the Limits of Law,* 83 MICH. L. REV. 1065, 1070–73 (1985).
6. *See* Plessy v. Ferguson, 163 U.S. 537, 551–52, 557, 560 (1896), discussed *supra* chapter 1, text at notes 1–15. *See also* Dimond & Sperling, *supra* note 5, at 1071 and n. 19.
7. Although Congress did *not* pass such legislation in response to the "massive resistance" movement that greeted the Court's rulings in *Brown* and *Bolling,* it has enacted a series of antibusing and so-called equal educational opportunity provisions, which just skirted the issue of trying to tell the Court how to interpret the meaning of the Constitution with respect to school segregation. *See, e.g.,* The Civil Rights Act of 1964, 42 U.S.C. 2000c-6 (no "racial balance"); Education Amendments of 1972, 20 U.S.C. 1651–56 (no "racial balance" and no use of federal funding for busing); 1974 Equal Educational Opportunities Act, 20 U.S.C. 1701–57 (pupil assignments "only to closest or next closest school," no "racial balance," delay any court-ordered busing until all appeals completed). The Court responded to all of these provisions by narrowly interpreting them as not intended to limit the Court's interpretation of the fifth and fourteenth amendments with respect to school segregation and any judicial decrees designed to remedy constitutional wrongs. *See, e.g.,* Swann v. Charlotte-Mecklenburg Board of Education, 402 U.S. 1, 17–18 (1971); Drummond v. Acree, 409 U.S. 1228 (Powell, J., in chambers, sitting as a single Circuit Justice to consider a school board's petition to stay a lower court's order until reviewed by the United States Supreme Court). This statutory gambit served the same function as the clear statement rule in giving Congress another chance to look at the issues without reaching any final constitutional questions.
8. 358 U.S. 1, 16 (1958).
9. *See* note 7 *supra*.
10. Brown II, 349 U.S. 294, 301 (1955).
11. Dimond & Sperling, *supra* note 4, at 1085–86 and n. 72; Sperling, *Judicial Right Declaration and Entrenched Discrimination,* 94 YALE L.J. 1743 (1985).
12. *See, e.g.,* Fiss, *The Forms of Justice,* 93 HARV. L. REV. 1 (1979).
13. *See, e.g.,* the discussion of the Delaware State Board of Education's openly discriminatory "reverse volunteerism" proposal in the Wilmington school case, whereby all blacks would be reassigned to white schools but then given the

opportunity to opt to transfer to their former black schools, but no whites would be reassigned or otherwise transferred. P. DIMOND, BEYOND BUSING 314–21 (1985).

14. *See, e.g.*, Dimond, *The Anti-Caste Principle*, 30 WAYNE L. REV. 1, 42–48 (1983); Dimond & Sperling, *supra* note 11, at 1084–86.

15. Unfortunately, the Burger Court did not take advantage of the opportunity that *Brown* afforded with respect both to declaring rights and to reviewing remedial proposals. Although the Burger Court purported on occasion to adopt such a judicial standard for reviewing remedial proposals, it did so primarily the context of "educational components," such as special reading programs for black students. The Court found that such relief ancillary to actual desegregation was designed to overcome the assumed educational harm resulting from intentional segregation. *See* Milliken v. Bradley, 433 U.S. 267 (1977). Read in the context of its attempts to avoid consideration of the wider-ranging proof of caste segregation itself (*See* P. DIMOND, BEYOND BUSING 171–80, 395–402 (1985)), the Burger Court's numerous rulings on desegregation suggest that a much different standard was in operation: the diverse factions on the Court became obsessed with the tension between (1) specifically tailoring any judicially decreed school desegregation remedy to no more than overcoming the direct effects of the most limited view of intentional segregation proven in the lower courts and (2) broadly ordering complete school desegregation relief by focusing on the depth of the particular wrongs committed specifically by school authorities. The failure to bifurcate consideration of the nature of the basic caste wrong at issue from remedy certainly contributed to this almost exclusive remedial focus, either on justifying or minimizing actual school desegregation relief. In the process, the Burger Court lost sight of its judicial responsibility, in the first instance, to examine the basic violation question: is the pervasive segregation of blacks from whites in schools, housing, and community life throughout metropolitan America the modern legacy of the prior regime of Jim Crow caste? *See* P. DIMOND, BEYOND BUSING 395–402 (1985); L. TRIBE, AMERICAN CONSTITUTIONAL LAW 1500, 1514–21 (1988); Dimond & Sperling, *Of Cultural Determinism and the Limits of Law*, 83 MICH. L. REV. 1065, 1083–86 (1985); Dimond, *Telling Government What's Right*, 3 YALE LAW & POLICY REVIEW 295, 302–06 (1984); Days, *School Desegregation in the 1980's*, 95 YALE 1737, 1761–68 (1986).

16. The Warren Court did just this in upholding the 1964 Civil Rights Act (*see* Heart of Atlanta Motel v. United States, 379 U.S. 241 (1964)) and the 1965 Voting Rights Act. *See* Katzenbach v. Morgan, 384 U.S. 64 (1966).

CHAPTER 6

Personal Autonomy and Abortion: Initiating a Dialogue over Individual Freedom from Government Intrusion

In the words of Charles Fairman, the privileges or immunities clause of the fourteenth amendment is "not static." Instead, it is "capable of sound development: those conditions to which one is entitled by virtue of being a citizen of the United States—the protection and dignity that are [the citizen's] due, the opportunities, associations and relationships that ought to be open to [the citizen]." Thus, "as the nation's experiences change . . . , surely the privilege of membership in this national community must broaden to include what has become essential under prevailing circumstances."[1] The Supreme Court has used just this conception of evolving fundamental values, but in the guise of interpreting the due process clause (and to a somewhat lesser extent the equal protection clause) substantively.[2]

These cases involve a variety of personal rights. The most controversial may relate to privacy and personal autonomy,[3] while the most confounding concern educational opportunity.[4] Chapter 6 first evaluates how the autonomy cases might evolve under provisional review, and then Chapter 7 discusses how the education cases might develop. Together, these two types of cases illustrate how provisional review could operate to promote an ongoing national dialogue over what it means to be a member of the national community under the Constitution.[5]

The most controversial of the personal autonomy cases arose when the Court chose to protect from governmental regulation the person's choice of whether to bear or beget a child.[6] *Roe v. Wade*, protecting the pregnant mother's choice of whether to bear the unborn child until the fetus is viable outside the womb, has been the center of this firestorm of public debate.[7]

Three types of criticism have been launched against *Roe*. First, the moral dilemma is stark and there are strong moral claims on both sides: the state may argue that aborting an unborn child is the equivalent of murder, while the woman can claim that compelling her against her will to put her body in the state's service for nine months to carry an unborn child to term amounts to involuntary servitude. Second, there is no *judicial* way for the Court to interpret the Constitution as protecting the moral claims of the woman over the state. Third, it is illegitimate for the Court to resolve this moral dilemma as an unelected final arbiter rather than leaving it to continuing resolution by the people in our representative democracy.

Provisional review may not completely answer, but it does deflect, all three of these objections. The Court's role in weighing and deciding between the conflicting claims is authorized by the privileges or immunities clause. The Court's procedures, methods, and reasoning are judicial and regularly used by the judiciary in a variety of noncontroversial contexts. And the Court's rulings are provisional rather than final, subject to continuing resolution by the people's representatives in Congress.[8]

The Court, in the first instance, accepts the *invitation* of the privileges or immunities clause of the fourteenth amendment to resolve just such substantive conflicts between the states and the individual by choosing to interpret what the Court thinks it means to be a member of the national community. Although the principle that the Court has developed to resolve this conflict in the case of abortion may not be based on the framer's intent and is not compelled by the text of the Constitution, it is a general principle with broad application: "whether one person's body should be the source of another life must be left to that person and that person alone to decide."[9]

This principle has roots in the even more general personal autonomy that Courts and legislatures have thrown up to protect what it means to be human from the seemingly ever more complex regulations and intrusions of government in modern life. Inevitably, in interpreting these privileges or immunities of a citizen in the national community, the Court does not define such national rights absolutely. Instead the Court must weigh the individual's claimed national privilege against the interests asserted by the states and articulate why (or why not) the individual's national claim should prevail against the state,[10] just as the Court does in refereeing other conflicts between state regulation and the individual's assertion of a conflicting federal interest in a variety of other contexts.* Finally, provi-

*Lawrence Tribe, perhaps the foremost proponent of the Supreme Court's declaration of fundamental values among the contemporary constitutional scholars, notes that the very form of the Court's "strict scrutiny," "compelling interest," and "intermediate review" standards inevitably results in a dialogue about what it means to be "human" as society evolves. The Court weighs the claimed governmental interest against its understanding of the fundamental value. Over time through this flexible process, there is a resonance between the people and the Court as both continue to evaluate and to debate the appropriate weight to be given to the personal versus the governmental interest. For Tribe, the purpose of this dialogue is "to encourage wise reflection" over what substantive values our society should hold fundamental. L. TRIBE, AMERICAN CONSTITUTIONAL LAW 1308 (1988). Justice Brennan has described this "evolutionary process" as an ongoing search for the "constitutional vision" of "human dignity" in our increasingly complex society. *See* Brennan speech, *reprinted in* FEDERALIST SOCIETY, THE GREAT DEBATE: IN-

sional review authorizes the Congress, where all of the people in the States are represented, to debate and to weigh the competing interests and claims independently and to legislate a different answer.

To understand the operation of provisional review, consider how a hypothetical, antiabortion Congress might respond to the Court's ruling in *Roe* under a substantive reading of the due process clause that the woman's right to choose for herself whether to bear or beget a child outweighed the state's interest in the life of the unborn child until the fetus was viable outside the mother's womb. Imagine that, after debating the issues, Congress responds with the "Right to Life Act of 1984." Its preamble provides, "There is no conflict between the interests of unborn children and their mothers. The paramount destiny and mission of woman, even more important than her duty to be a good wife to her man, is to fulfill the noble and beneficent office of mother. That is the law of nature and of her Creator." The preamble concludes, "There is a conflict between the life of the unborn child and the life of the mother, however, when the life of the mother will be seriously threatened if the pregnancy is not aborted."

Due to the fears of a majority in Congress that some states might pass laws allowing women to choose abortions in other circumstances, the substantive provisions of the Act provide for the President to appoint a Pro-Life Board to promulgate binding regulations "to prohibit any person subject to the laws of the United States from choosing, performing, aiding, or abetting an abortion except when the life or health of the mother will be placed in jeopardy if the pregnancy is not aborted." The Act also gives the Attorney General the authority to seek injunctions to enforce the Act and to prosecute any person who violates the Act; the maximum penalty is set at nine months for any mother having an abortion and life imprisonment for any person performing, aiding, or abetting an abortion. The Pro-Life Board then passes a regulation defining all abortions as unlawful under the Act, "except those required to protect the life of the mother from clear and present danger of death as certified by a physician approved by this Board to make such decisions."

Imagine that a woman who is suffering a very difficult, but not imminently life-threatening pregnancy, feels that she cannot accept the burdens of pregnancy. She consults her personal physician and several specialists; together they decide that she needs an abortion to avoid crippling (but not life-threatening) injury that probably will result if she carries the

---

TERPRETING OUR WRITTEN CONSTITUTION 11–25 (1986). Provisional review would utilize a similar form of discourse by the Court; but in most cases, the people could respond through ordinary legislation in Congress to the Court's elaboration of the individual's personal rights of substance as weighed against conflicting governmental interests.

baby to term. The woman therefore requests and her personal physician provides an abortion. Both are prosecuted and convicted under the Act and appeal their convictions to the United States Supreme Court.

On review, the Court could overturn the convictions by invalidating the regulation promulgated by the Pro-Life Board. In pertinent part the Court's opinion might reason,

> The Pro-Life Board's regulation does not implement the substantive provisions of the Act. In particular, as applied to the facts of this case, the regulation seeks to make it a crime for a woman to elect not to bear a fetus even though she would have suffered crippling injuries if she had carried the fetus to term. The Act, however, excepts from its prohibitions just such situations "when the . . . health of the mother will be placed in jeopardy if the pregnancy is not aborted." The Board exceeded the limits of the law enacted by Congress, and the regulation is therefore void. Indeed, it is not clear from the substantive provisions of the Act to what extent, if any, Congress intended national policy to differ from the standards set forth in *Roe v. Wade*. Until Congress establishes a controlling policy, which if Congress so elects is implemented by lawful regulations of a federal agency, laws of the several states, or statutory standards capable of application by the judiciary, women shall continue to have the same right to choose an abortion against any conflicting state regulation as set forth in our earlier ruling in *Roe v. Wade*.

The Court adds three pointed observations. First,

> In establishing policy where constitutional interests are implicated, the Congress must decide the merits of the issues clearly and directly. If Congress chooses to delegate implementation of that clearly stated national policy to a federal agency or the states, this Court will review agency regulations and state laws carefully to assure that they do not subvert the national policy enacted by Congress.

Second,

> In resolving this case by statutory construction of the Act, we avoid serious constitutional issues raised by the process of lawmaking of the Right to Life Act. The preamble to the Act raises serious concerns that the Act may have been passed out of such deep prejudice against women that the interests of women as individual persons were virtually ignored. In particular, the preamble appears to be based on the antiquated male supremacy myth that a woman

is fit only to be a mother and therefore bears no burdens if forced to bear a child against her will. Given the concern expressed in other legislation throughout the nation for government not compelling persons to be good samaritans by bearing much smaller burdens against their will to save the life of another, it is difficult to understand how the unique burdens born by an unwilling mother compelled by law to bear a child could be totally ignored unless the lawmaking process was blinded by prejudice against women.[11] If this Court were to find that such a caste-based defect actually influenced the congressional lawmaking process, there would be serious questions whether such a law conflicts with the due process of law guaranteed by the fifth amendment. Because of our ruling today, Congress will have the opportunity to reconsider the merits of the substantive issues before it and weigh carefully the interests of the unborn child in life against the woman's interest in controlling her own body free from the burdens of government compelling her to bear a child against her will.

Third,

The extent to which Congress is prohibited by a substantive reading of the due process clause of the fifth amendment from regulating a woman's right to choose an abortion under the *Roe* guidelines raises grave constitutional concerns. The integrity of this Court's power of final judicial review, the meaning of the fifth amendment's due process clause, and the constitutional limits on the substance of congressional power would then be at issue. A constitutional confrontation of the first order between the Congress and this Court is therefore avoided by our narrow interpretation of the statute.

In a series of orders without opinions issued the same day, the Court summarily reverses over 60,000 convictions of women who have aborted their pregnancies and of 2,000 physicians who conducted the operations. In each of these cases, the fetus had been aborted within the first eight weeks of pregnancy on the basis of consultation between the women and their physicians. In each, the decision had been made to abort the fetus on the grounds that bearing the burdens of an unwanted pregnancy would hurt the mental health and well-being of the mother.*

*One can imagine a dissent by the Chief Justice in the following terms:

The Congress is entitled to delegate implementation of its duly enacted laws to federal agencies. The only standard of review is whether the agency's regulation reasonably implements congressional intent. The preamble makes clear that Congress intended only to permit abortions if the life of the mother was

To continue this hypothetical exploration, imagine that Congress responds to this decision by debating abortion for several years, and it becomes one of the major issues in the next presidential campaign. Imagine that a pro-life president is then elected who, upon the deaths of four of the Associate Justices of the Supreme Court, appoints four pro-life Justices

---

seriously threatened, and the Pro-Life Board's regulation reasonably implements this intent. If Congress has changed its mind or wishes to overturn the board's regulation, it remains free to do so without this Court essentially invalidating a lawful pro-life policy duly enacted by the people's representatives in Congress.

But even if the regulation as applied to this case were deemed invalid, the regulation is clearly valid in each of the other cases summarily reversed by the Court this day. There is not even the slightest suggestion of any serious injury, let alone a threat to life, in any of these cases. There is no reason to permit these convicted felons to throw out all the babies because this Court believes that the mothers' well-being may have been inconvenienced by the natural burdens of child-bearing, for which women are well-equipped. The Court's tortured construction of the statute to avoid constitutional issues will not atone for the evils condoned this day.

Moreover, each of the physicians who performed or abetted these abortions refused even to seek approval from the Pro-Life Board to review the mothers' decisions. These doctors took a Hippocratic oath to preserve life; instead, they act like hypocrites, lying to justify murder. They are criminals today, just as much as Al Capone was during Prohibition. They hide behind white coats and medical degrees: but their weapons of abortion are far more deadly than guns, and their associations of doctors far more powerful than the mob. These so-called medical doctors should be denied standing to challenge their convictions because they refused even to consult with the Pro-Life Board.

The *dictum* of the Court on sexism, albeit gratuitous, also calls for a response. We all know the difficulties of proving racial intent. We also know the dangers of requiring legislatures to think in racial terms; that is why I have argued that the fifth and fourteenth amendment guarantees against discrimination should be limited to race and should be controlled by a strict standard of color-blindness. The defeat of the Equal Rights Amendment confirms that sex bias, no matter how unfortunate, is of no relevance to this Court under the Constitution as written in reviewing legislative acts or other official decisions. Indeed, the Court's invitation to Congress to examine the special circumstances of women would only interfere with congressional consideration of the basic moral question at issue: is abortion wrong except when the life of the child-bearer is clearly threatened?

Finally, this Court should reach the basic constitutional issue: should the due process clauses be read substantively to restrict the power of Congress to prohibit abortion? My answer is an unequivocal no. If anything, the due process clauses should be read substantively to prohibit the states and the Congress from interfering with the right of the unborn child to life, except when the life of the mother will be placed in serious jeopardy by continuing the child-bearing to birth.

who are openly committed to joining the dissenting Chief Justice on the Supreme Court in overruling *Roe v. Wade*. Also, suppose there is a state that, in response to the Court's original ruling in *Roe v. Wade,* previously had established state centers to provide abortions on demand to any woman at state expense during the first trimester. A husband who wants to contest his wife's decision to have an abortion at a state center brings suit in federal court for injunctive relief by claiming that his equal right to have the child under the privileges or immunities clause of the fourteenth amendment would be violated. As guardian for the unborn child whom his wife wants to abandon, he further argues that the unborn child's interest in life will be deprived, without due process of law, if the state center is allowed to perform the abortion. Assume that the trial court enjoins the center from performing the abortion and the mother from having the abortion, pending review by the Supreme Court of the husband's claims. The trial court reasons, "I can count. There are now five votes on the Supreme Court, enough not only to reverse *Roe,* but also to substitute a new rule requiring the states to protect the life of the unborn child unless the pregnancy or impending childbirth will imperil the life of the mother. This unborn child deserves the chance to live to enjoy the benefits of that ruling."

On review in the Supreme Court, the trial court's prediction is confirmed, in part, by a 5 to 4 vote. Led by the Chief Justice, four members of the Court reason that the husband has a national privilege to assure that the state does not abridge his right to the birth of his child, and that "the husband's right clearly outweighs the mother's interest in killing the baby." These Justices also argue, "The unborn child is a person under the due process clause of the fourteenth amendment whose life the state may not permit to be taken by anyone under any circumstances other than when the life of the mother is clearly in danger unless the pregnancy is aborted."

The fifth, and deciding, vote comes from one of the newly appointed pro-life Justices. But she bases her decision solely on the privileges or immunities clause. She argues,

> The due process clause should be limited to the fair process its language reflects. As a consequence, Congress will then be able to enact a different national policy free from fear that this Court will strike it down by a substantive reading of the due process clause of the fifth amendment, at least so long as the national process of lawmaking focuses clearly on the issue and is not tainted by any caste-based defects.

Her opinion concludes,

> Although I believe strongly that the life of the unborn child should be protected under all circumstances, I believe just as strongly in

> the importance of the people having the power to decide such substantive values of national importance through their elected representatives in Congress. When *Roe v. Wade* was originally decided, I disagreed with the result on moral grounds; but I was also troubled by the apparent claim that the Court should be the final arbiter of such moral judgments simply because it chose to read the due process clause substantively. I do not think that the Constitution as written necessarily gives the Court the final word on such value judgments. To the contrary, the Court can initiate a dialogue with the people over what it means to be a member of the national community that constitutes these United States by accepting the Constitution's invitation to interpret the privileges or immunities clause of the fourteenth amendment with respect to state action. That will leave it up to the people, through their representatives in Congress, to continuously resolve these questions for themselves. I am convinced that resolution of such substantive issues of national rights should not depend on how long the Justices who originally decided cases like *Dred Scott, Lochner, Roe,* and this case happen to live.

The four dissenters concur in this opinion insofar as it relates to the structure of provisional review, but dissent on the ground that a woman has the national privilege to choose whether to bear a child until the fetus is viable outside the womb.

Imagine that at the next congressional election, a compromise coalition sweeps the House races and wins enough seats to secure the support of two-thirds of the Senators. Over the President's veto, this coalition passes the "Pro-Life, Pro-Mother Act of 1992." Its preamble notes,

> For too long, the pro-life advocates have refused to recognize that women bear unique burdens when they bear children, burdens that no man can fully share let alone bear. These unique burdens are compounded if the government tells a woman that she must bear a child against her will. For too long, the pro-choice advocates have refused to recognize that the unborn child has a moral claim to life, which may even be greater than that of the woman to control of her own body, at least until her life or health are placed at risk. The Congress has resolved, insofar as possible, to protect the life of the unborn child, except when the continuation of the pregnancy seriously threatens the life or the health of the mother. The Congress has also resolved, insofar as possible, to protect pregnant women from discrimination generally, to compensate unwilling mothers for the costs of childbearing specifically, and to promote conditions that will allow all women, and particularly new mothers, to advance into the mainstream of economic, business, social, and political life in America.

The substantive provisions of the act include, among others:

1. A prohibition against having, performing, or aiding in an abortion except upon the request of the mother and the certification of two licensed physicians that the pregnancy seriously threatens the life or health of the mother. This prohibition is enforcible by injunctions, as well as by criminal actions punishable by a maximum of three months of alternative service in a pediatric ward, abortion clinic, or daycare center.

2. An affirmative action program to provide mothers with pregnancy leaves from employment extending up to one year after birth at full pay and with full advancement upon return from leaves, with similar paid leaves for fathers who take responsibility for child rearing for the first year after birth. The act permits part-time paid leaves for mothers and fathers who wish to share child-rearing responsibilities during the first year after birth.

3. Federally funded day-care facilities near the homes or jobs of working parents.

4. An anticaste program to outlaw discrimination against women in employment, recreational and social clubs, professional organizations, and business roundtables; and to promote the advancement of women and mothers in all of these areas of business and community life. A federal agency is established to review, approve, and oversee implementation of plans submitted by the states, private employers, clubs, and associations to implement this program. The Attorney General and interested individuals are given the right to bring civil suit for injunctive or damage relief to enforce the provisions of any approved plan or to challenge the decision of the federal agency.

5. A compensation board with funding to pay for the costs (*a*) of childbearing, including damages for the burdens imposed on any woman forced to bear a child against her will, and (*b*) of approved abortions.

6. A nationwide program to compel all fathers, whether married, separated, single, or divorced to provide either monetary support or parenting for all of their children, backed up by a national parental support insurance pool financed by a new children's security tax of $1000 levied upon the divorce of every couple able to pay.

7. Funding for state adoption agencies and foster care programs so that no mother will be compelled against her will to care for the infant after birth.

This Pro-Life, Pro-Mother Act may not offer the right answer to the conflicting claims in the abortion debate. But is there any doubt that the five members of the hypothetical Court who supported provisional review would be disposed to reject most challenges to this Act? As to the resolution of the conflicting interests of women and unborn children, provisional review invites the people, through their representatives in Congress, to resolve this substantive issue. As to the process of lawmaking, a sensitive inquiry into the legislative history of the Act is essential. On its face, however, the Act appears honestly to recognize the interests of women in control over their own bodies and to try to accommodate that interest insofar as the conflicting interest of the unborn child permits. In addition, the Act attempts to compensate for the unique burdens of childbearing and to address the wide-ranging effects of any resulting caste system of discrimination against women in the workplace and community life. Unless a plaintiff challenging the Act proves that such provisions are just pretextual window dressing for a congressional law-making process that has been tainted by caste discrimination against women, the five members of the hypothetical Court committed to provisional review should uphold the Act.

Assume, therefore, that the Court upholds the constitutionality of the Pro-Life, Pro-Mother Act. During the next decade women make real progress in business, community, and political life as the pro-women provisions of the Act spur women (and men) and the entire nation to take full advantage of the skills and resources offered by women, including mothers. During this period, however, women of means begin by the millions to take a home abortion pill manufactured in Sweden and smuggled into the United States. This pill, if taken within the first month of conception enables women with the necessary wherewithal to terminate their pregnancies immediately with no adverse side effects to the woman. At the same time, many poor and uninformed women either bear children they do not want to mother or seek relatively unsafe operations from underground abortion clinics with a high incidence of serious injury to the pregnant mothers. Nevertheless, the pro-mother and pro-women provisions of the Act do lead to an increase in the birth rates for mothers in middle- and upper-income families.

In response to these developments, imagine that a new Congress repeals the pro-life aspects of the prior Act in passing the "Pro-Choice Act of 2002." The preamble of the Act states:

> Given the interests of women in the control over their own bodies and in the decision on whether to bear a child, Congress determines that all women, whether rich or poor, should have access to the pregnancy diagnostic test and, if they so choose, the safe and effective abortion pill. It is a national scandal that women without means or information have been forced underground to unsafe abortion clinics that butcher the unsuspecting mother while aborting the unborn child. Equally troublesome, the Pro-Life Act has attempted to make criminals out of all of the millions of women who have chosen abortions over the past decade. The deci-

> sion on whether to bear or beget a child is a very private decision, to be made by each person. No matter how deeply some in our country might want to prohibit the choice of any woman not to bear a child in the interests of preserving the unborn's life, that is a choice that each person must make as her own conscience dictates. As a nation, we are better served by a pro-choice, pro-mother policy.

To implement this congressional determination, the substantive provisions repeal the prior Act's prohibition against abortions and continue the pregnancy and early child-rearing leaves, day-care support, child support, pro-women and pro-mother affirmative programs, adoption and foster care funding, and the compensation board to pay for the costs of pregnancy and childbirth (or of the abortion pill) if the mother chooses.

Under provisional review we the people, through our representatives in Congress, may continuously resolve such substantive questions for ourselves. Any Justice of the Supreme Court committed to this framework for judicial review would also uphold the Pro-Choice Act of 2002, whatever her prior interpretation of the meaning of the privileges or immunities clause of the fourteenth amendment as against the states with respect to abortion. Under our hypothetical Court, we may therefore safely assume that a majority of the Court would uphold this Act, led by the Associate Justice who had overruled *Roe v. Wade* under the privileges or immunities rather than the due process clause.

In the alternative Congress could have enacted a State Choice Act on Bearing Children, in 1984, 1992, or 2002, rather than the right to life, pro-life, pro-mother, or pro-choice acts described in the text. Such a State Choice Act could authorize each state to establish its own policy in weighing the interest of the woman in determining whether to bear a child against the life of the unborn child. If this State Choice Act were premised on the notion that the states should decide the abortion issues because women are not deserving of respect and concern as individuals and have *no* interest in determining whether to bear or beget a child, the Court could invalidate this Act on anticaste grounds. On the other hand, if Congress recognized the conflicting interests but wanted each state to make its own choice so long as the state's own law-making process was not tainted by antiwomen bias, the Court would uphold this national State Choice Act under provisional review.

The diverse responses of the states to such national legislation would still be subject to review by the Court to assure that the state lawmaking process is free from caste-based defects under the equal protection clause of the fourteenth amendment. Thus, the Court could continue the dialogue with the people over the abortion issue in response to specific laws enacted by each state. For example, assume that one state passed a Right to Life Act, another state passed a Pro-Life, Pro-Mother Act, and a third state passed a Pro-Choice, Pro-Mother Act, all three with the same terms and provisions as the national Acts described in the text. Under provisional review, the Court could invalidate the first state's Right to Life Act on the ground that its enactment had been infected by caste discrimination against women, while upholding the two other states' Pro-Choice, Pro-Mother and Pro-Life, Pro-Mother Acts. The substantive decision over the abortion issue would remain in the hands of the people, through their elected representatives in each state, but the process of legislating the substantive decision would still be subject to review by the Court.

The point of all of these hypotheticals is to illustrate how the Court could move to adopt provisional review and thereby promote an ongoing dialogue with the people over what the privilege of membership in our national community means for each generation in contemporary America. Having posited a national privilege—whether the right of the unborn child to life or the right of the woman to choose whether to bear or to abort the unborn child—under section 1 of the fourteenth amendment, the Court does not necessarily have the final word. The people, through their representatives in Congress, may enact legislation under section 8 of article I providing a different answer. The Court will then review such national legislation to make sure that it focuses on the merits of these issues of vital national importance and is not infected by caste discrimination (here by men against women).

NOTES

1. C. FAIRMAN, RECONSTRUCTION AND REUNION 1388 (1971). *See also, id.* at 1297; C. FAIRMAN, RECONSTRUCTION AND REUNION, PART II (1987).
2. *See* chapter 2 *supra,* text at note 43; and Introduction *supra,* text at and notes 17–22 and 63; G. GUNTHER, CONSTITUTIONAL LAW 588–89, 787–853. (1985).
3. *Compare, e.g.,* L. TRIBE, AMERICAN CONSTITUTIONAL LAW 1302–1435 (1988) with J. ELY, DEMOCRACY AND DISTRUST 43–72 (1980).
4. *Compare,* San Antonio Independent School District v. Rodriguez, 411 U.S. 1 (1973) *with* Plyler v. Doe, 457 U.S. 202 (1982).
5. Rulings seeking to provide a few islands of refuge in an ocean of free market competition used to provide another primary strand of this substantive development of the constitutional meaning of personhood. Whether couched in the rubric of discrimination (usually against the poor) under the equal protection clause or fundamental fairness under due process analysis (*compare* Griffin v. Illinois, 351 U.S. 12 (1956) *with* Boddie v. Connecticut, 401 U.S. 371 (1971)), the support for such "minimum protection" waned in the Burger Court and runs the risk of being even further shriveled. *Compare, e.g.,* Michelman, *On Protecting the Poor through the Fourteenth Amendment,* 83 HARV. L. REV. 7 (1969) *with* Dandridge v. Williams, 397 U.S. 471 (1970); James v. Valtierra, 402 U.S. 137 (1971); Lindsey v. Normet 405 U.S. 56 (1972); United States v.

Kras, 409 U.S. 434 (1973); and Lassiter v. Department of Social Services, 452 U.S. 18 (1981). *See also,* L. TRIBE, AMERICAN CONSTITUTIONAL LAW 1625–72 (1988). Although beyond the scope of the personhood cases discussed in chapters 6 and 7, provisional review could also authorize the Court to stimulate a national dialogue over the minimum protection owed to every member of the national community under the Constitution in these cases as well. *Cf also* the discussion, *supra,* chapter 4, of self-actualization and nonpolitical expression cases, which also might thrive under a provisional review approach to free speech cases.

6. *See, e.g.,* Skinner v. Oklahoma, 316 U.S. 535 (1942) (striking down state-compelled sterilization); Griswold v. Connecticut, 381 U.S. 479 (1965) (invalidating a statute prohibiting use of contraceptives by married persons); Eisenstadt v. Baird, 405 U.S. 438 (1972) (holding unconstitutional a state measure making contraceptives less available to unmarried than married persons).
7. *Compare* Roe v. Wade, 410 U.S. 113 (1973), *with* Ely, *The Wages of Crying Wolf,* 83 YALE L.J. 221 (1973), and L. TRIBE, *supra* note 3, at 1349 n.80 and 1352 n.99 (discussing the ruling of the West German Constitutional Court invalidating laws permitting abortions in the first trimester and holding that a state has an affirmative duty to protect the unborn child from abortion except when continuation of the pregnancy would gravely imperil the woman's life or health).
8. *See, e.g,* Summers, *Two Types of Substantive Reasons: The Core of a Theory of Common-Law Justification,* 63 CORNELL L. REV. 707 (1978); G. CALABRESI, A COMMON LAW FOR THE AGE OF STATUTES (1982). *See also* Fiss, *The Forms of Justice,* 93 HARV. L. REV. 1 (1979); Sandalow, *Constitutional Interpretation,* 79 MICH. L. REV. 1033 (1978); Wellington, *The Nature of Judicial Review,* 91 YALE L.J. 486 (1982); and R. DWORKIN, TAKING RIGHTS SERIOUSLY (1978).
9. L. TRIBE, *supra* note 3, at 1340.
10. *See* chapter 2 *supra.*
11. *Cf.* Regan, *Rewriting Roe v. Wade,* 77 MICH. L. REV 1569 (1979); Skinner v. Oklahoma, 326 U.S. 535 (1942); L. TRIBE, AMERICAN CONSTITUTIONAL LAW 1354, 1463–65, 1577–85 (1988).

CHAPTER 7

Education and Judicial Review: Initiating a Dialogue over the Government's Responsibility to Provide Basic Opportunity to All Persons

If abortion has provided the most controversial of the personhood cases, education offers the most confounding. In contrast to the personal autonomy cases where the Court is asked only to tell government to stop intruding on the individual, the education cases ask the Court to order the government to make a particular service or benefit available to all persons. Although education is almost always touted as perhaps the most important governmental function for the development of the individual and for the health of our society, education standing alone has never achieved any such special status in the Court's interpretation of the Constitution. Indeed, education is much like a chameleon: whatever status it does achieve derives from the company it keeps; and its camouflage is often so good that it sometimes seems to masquerade as an independent constitutional right.

For example, in *Brown v. Board of Education,* Chief Justice Warren went out of his way to explain that education had grown from a relatively small enterprise for a privileged few when the fourteenth amendment was adopted in 1868 into

> perhaps the most important function of state and local governments. Compulsory school attendance laws and the great expenditures for education both demonstrate our recognition of the importance of education to our democratic society. It is required in the performance of the most basic public responsibilities, even service in the armed forces. It is the very foundation of good citizenship. Today, it is a principal instrument in awakening the child to cultural values, in preparing him for later professional training, and in helping him to adjust normally to his environment. In these days, it is doubtful that any child may reasonably be expected to succeed in life if he is denied the opportunity of an education.

The Chief Justice added: "Such an opportunity, where the State has undertaken to provide it, is a right which must be made available to all on equal terms."

Indeed, Warren framed the issue in the case in just these terms:

"Does segregation of children in public schools solely on the basis of race, even though the physical facilities and other 'tangible factors' may be equal, deprive the children of the minority group of equal educational opportunities? We believe that it does." Warren proceeded to drive this point home in the most human terms by focusing on the harm to the plaintiff black schoolchildren: "To separate them from others of similar age and qualifications solely because of their race generates a feeling of inferiority as to their status in the community that may affect their hearts and minds in a way unlikely ever to be undone."[1]

Warren's phrasing no doubt caused much of the confusion about an independent constitutional right to "equal educational opportunity." As we have seen, however, *Brown* is a case about race, not education.[2] Its progeny prohibited state-enforced segregation in all public services rather than promoting educational opportunities for all in a variety of circumstances. At issue was the caste system of segregation by which the white majority subjugated the black minority to a subordinate status, not whether blacks or whites learned better in segregated or integrated schools.

In *San Antonio Independent School District v. Rodriguez,* the Burger Court considered the constitutionality of state school finance systems based on local school district property taxes. In Texas, as elsewhere, this method of financing public schooling produced wildly varying per pupil expenditures throughout the state, depending on the relative per pupil property wealth of the local districts. By a 5 to 4 vote, the Court determined that such state school finance schemes do not violate the Constitution. While quoting verbatim Chief Justice Warren's encomium in *Brown* to education, Justice Powell proceeded for the majority to note that "the importance of a service performed by the State does not determine whether it must be regarded as fundamental for purposes of examination" under the fourteenth amendment.[3] The "key to discovering whether education is 'fundamental' is not to be found in comparisons of the relative societal significance of education as opposed to subsistence or housing,"[4] or minimum levels of health care for that matter. For Justice Powell, "the answer lies in assessing whether there is a right to education explicitly or implicitly guaranteed in the Constitution".[5] Justice Powell concluded, "education, of course, is not among the rights afforded explicit protection under our Federal Constitution. Nor do we find any basis for saying it is implicitly so protected".[6]

Despite the Court's continuing recognition of the importance of education, it was as irrelevant to the Court's decision in *Rodriguez* as in *Brown*. Indeed, *Rodriguez* was not really a case about education at all. As in *Brown,* it merely provided what plaintiffs hoped would be an appealing setting for challenging what they deemed to be invidious forms of discrimination, racial in *Brown* and fiscal in *Rodriguez*.[7] Fiscal discrimination, however, proved to be such an unsympathetic breeding ground for the development of federal constitutional doctrine that both the plaintiffs and the Court confused the issue and treated it much as discrimination against poor persons when there was no real proof that poor persons were necessarily clustered within school districts with lower per pupil property wealth.[8] Whatever the confusion, Justice Powell concluded that state school finance schemes founded on local district property wealth do not discriminate against any suspect class and that any such wealth discrimination standing alone does not require the Court to strictly scrutinize the underlying classification with respect to education.[9]

In *Plyler v. Doe,* however, the Court by a similarly narrow 5 to 4 vote ruled unconstitutional a Texas law that barred illegal alien children from the free public education provided in Texas public schools to U.S. citizens and lawfully admitted aliens. While conceding that education is not a fundamental personal right guaranteed by the Constitution, Justice Brennan argued that education is not "merely some governmental 'benefit' indistinguishable from other forms of social welfare legislation." He proceeded to catalog the diverse ways in which education is of critical importance to the development and well-being of the individual: it "provides the basic tools by which individuals might lead economically productive lives . . . [and] it prepares individuals to be self-reliant and self-sufficient participants in society." By depriving the individual of the opportunity of an education, Texas imposes the "enduring disability" of illiteracy on the child "each and every day of his life." At the same time, education plays "a fundamental role in maintaining the fabric of our society. . . . We cannot ignore the significant social costs borne by our Nation when select groups are denied the means to absorb the values and skills upon which our social order rests." Justice Brennan ended his paean to education by noting, "What we said 28 years ago in [*Brown*] still holds true: Today, education is perhaps the most important function of state and local governments."[10]

While conceding that discrimination against a class of illegal aliens is not necessarily suspect, Justice Brennan noted that the children hardly could be held accountable for their parents' choice to violate national immigration law. Indeed, by the operation of that same national immigration law, many of these children (and their children) might become lawful resident aliens or United States citizens. To the state's claim that it should be able to target its scarce resources on educating lawfully resident children, the majority on the Court countered with the spectre of the state perpetuating "a subclass of illiterates," "a permanent caste of undocumented resident aliens," and a "discrete underclass."[11] In this sense, the exclusion of this group of children from public schooling may also best be understood as a violation of the anticaste principle rather than as a violation of any constitutional right to education. As Laurence Tribe notes under his similar antisubjugation principle, "if equality under law means anything, it surely means that the government may not treat the helpless children of illegal aliens as untouchable and condemn them to lives of peonage."[12] On the other hand, there can be no doubt that the Court's novel ruling in *Plyler* was at least partially inspired because the caste discrimination arose in the context of public schooling. Unlike *Brown,* it is not clear that the Court would hold discrimination against undocumented alien children unconstitutional with respect to other government services (e.g., welfare, public housing, or health care).

One possible explanation for the Court's willingness to tout education without giving it much constitutional protection rests with the limits of final judicial review. If the Court is viewed as having the final word on the provision of governmental services such as education, then the specter of government by the judiciary rather than by the people's elected representatives grows. Understandably, a Court that seeks to act as if it has the final word will be very chary about exercising its authority to give an expansive interpretation to the meaning of the Constitution, particularly with respect to how the people choose through their state legislatures to raise and to spend money for all variety of government services. Indeed, as the costs of education continue to grow while the benefits resulting from the seemingly ever-increasing education expenditures are increasingly questioned, the Court may become even *less* inclined to enter this morass. The issue remains whether a Court that operates within the framework of provisional review might act any differently.

To explore this question, imagine a hypothetical 1992 Florida "Retirement-Vocation-Education Priority Act." The State of Florida passes this act in response to a coalition of business and retirement groups seeking (1) to reduce the total state and local tax burden on the growing retirement population and businesses and (2) to spend more on health care, housing, and recreation for the elderly and job training for businesses. The Act reduces the total state and local taxes on the average by one quarter by eliminating virtually all public support for schooling after the eighth grade, except for the talented fifth of the school population who demonstrate by a Florida skills and aptitude test that they are most likely to be able to benefit from a college education. These qualifying students are assigned to a series of state regional excellence schools that provide college preparatory education in grades nine through twelve. In addition to lowering the compulsory school age to fourteen years of age and cutting local school taxes by one-third, the Act requires that the local elementary school districts make available only basic skills training in English, math, and computer literacy for at least five hours each day for 180 school days for all children ages five through fourteen. The Act also provides (1) tax credits to employers to operate job training programs certified by the state; (2) tax credits to parents for sending their non-college-bound children to private vocational schools certified by the state; (3) a lowering of the age for work permits to fifteen; (4) a state-funded job corps, in conjunction with participating businesses to serve approximately 20 percent of the non-college-bound youths who do not participate in state-certified vocational schools or job training programs.

Finally, the Act creates a decentralized system of Retirement Districts with power to levy up to one-quarter of the property tax and bonding authority freed up by the lowering of local school taxes. At the same time, ownership of all of the unused senior high schools (and their playing fields) is transferred from the local school districts to the local retirement boards. The local retirement boards are authorized to use the former school buildings and grounds, and their new taxing and bonding authority, to make comprehensive health care, recreation, and congregate living programs and facilities available to retired persons over the age of fifty-five residing within their local districts.

In 1994 eight fifteen-year-old children who did not qualify for the state's publicly supported college preparatory high schools challenge the Florida Act on the grounds that it abridges their privileges or immunities as citizens of the United States under the fourteenth amendment. The eight plaintiffs include (1) a blind child of poor parents with an IQ of 140 who cannot pass the Florida skills and aptitude test because she cannot read but could do so with even one year of publicly financed specialized training; (2) a severely dyslexic child who could learn how to read and to communicate with another two years of special skills training; (3) a Spanish-speaking child of a Chicano migrant worker who cannot read or write because she never understood what was being said or written in the basic elementary education where English was the only language spoken, written, or read; (4) an illiterate, borderline-retarded child who could learn to read and to write with four more years of basic training: (5) an Anglo girl of poor parents who scored in the seventy-ninth percentile on Florida's college qualifying test, could not afford the tuition for private schooling, but had such unique skills in music that she would be accepted on a scholarship to any college of her choice if she could only obtain a high school degree; (6) a six-foot, four-inch, 150-pound, agile white daughter of poor parents who scored in the seventy-fifth percentile on Florida's college qualifying test but could not afford to pay for the college preparatory schooling necessary to enable her to enter virtually any Division I college on a basketball scholarship; (7) a black orphan who is functionally illiterate but could learn to read, to write, and to communicate with four more years of education; and (8) a poor black child who scored in the seventy-ninth percentile on Florida's college prep qualifying test but could not afford to pay tuition for the private high school education that would enable him to enter virtually any college in the country.

After hearing several weeks of testimony and reviewing the voluminous evidence produced in support of the plaintiff children and in defense of the state, the trial judge rules that the Act violates the privileges or immunities of the plaintiff children to a minimally adequate state-supported education through the age of seventeen. The district court stays any injunctive relief pending appellate review. On appeal, the court of appeals affirms but continues to stay any injunction pending review by the Supreme Court. The plaintiffs make no claim that the Act is tainted by a lawmaking process whose purpose or effect is to relegate any group or class to a subordinate status. Nevertheless, a first argument before the Supreme Court is so inconclusive that a closely divided Court asks for a second reargument focusing on a single issue—to what extent, if any, is the opportunity of publicly supported education a privilege or immunity of citizenship under the fourteenth amendment.

In its briefs and arguments the state demonstrates conclusively that the framers of the fourteenth amendment never in their wildest dreams considered secondary education such a privilege or immunity. In addition, the state argues that the Act is an innovative response to (*a*) the continuing decline in the effectiveness of traditional public education during the latter half of the twentieth century, (*b*) the needs of the growing elderly population that continues to migrate to Florida as the twenty-first century approaches, and (*c*) the demands for cuts in state and local taxes.

The plaintiffs demonstrate just as conclusively that the privileges or immunities clause was not intended by the framers to have a specific code meaning for all time; instead, the framers adopted general language that was capable of growth as the nation evolved over time. In addition, the plaintiffs argue that the Florida Act deprives some of the basic skills necessary to exercise their constitutional rights of free speech, petitioning their government for redress of grievances, and voting, while others are denied any meaningful opportunity to advance themselves through publicly supported secondary education, to college and professional schools, and on to the full opportunities and responsibilities of life in America in the twenty-first century.

For purposes of analysis, visualize the conference of the Justices in the chambers of the United States Supreme Court following the reargument. Imagine that the aging Chief Justice is striving to achieve the support of all the Justices for a unanimous opinion striking down the Act. Recall that the Chief Justice had previously refused to join the separate opinion by the swing vote in the abortion cases overturning *Roe v. Wade* and upholding the Pro-Life, Pro-Mother Act of 1992 under the operation of provisional review. The Chief Justice had always reasoned that the unborn child should be finally protected under a substantive reading of the due process clauses. On the other hand, he never had accepted some of his brethren's antiquated notions that women were fit *only* to be mothers and wives; his own wife and daughters had long since rendered that male chauvinist assumption untenable. The experience of his own grandchildren thereafter in taking abortion pills in private in violation of the Pro-Life Act to terminate unwanted pregnancy only added to his doubts about his own antiabortion stand. The Chief Justice has come to believe that the country will eventually move to make such safe and effective birth control available to all women on grounds of simple equity regardless of the moral claims of the unborn child to life. Nevertheless, he remains grateful that the Pro-Mother provisions of the 1992 Act are working to increase the number of women, especially women in middle- and upper-income households, bearing children. Perhaps, he thinks, it is time to reconsider his own view of the role of the Court in interpreting substantive rights under the Constitution. Perhaps provisional review reflects the reality of what the Court's role can and should be in the long course of history.

As the Chief Justice ponders the Florida Act, he sees just the first of many state laws that will reallocate resources from the education of the children of the country to the care, feeding, and housing of the elderly. As a matter of public policy, he views this as a prescription for the ultimate decline of the United States in the world: the elderly, who already have by far the highest per capita wealth in the country plus the added income provided by Social Security, are really flexing their Gray Panther muscles at the expense of the investment in young people necessary to give the country any chance to compete in the global marketplace in the twenty-first century. On the other hand, the Chief Justice recognizes that the growing expressions of concern about the failings of traditional public schooling are legitimate. He does not believe that cutting off 80 percent of the children over the age of fourteen from the opportunity of any meaningful state-supported educational opportunity provides any kind of answer.

As he listens to the comments of the other Justices around the conference table, he concludes that this case will be as important to the future of the country as *Brown* and *Plessy* and *Lochner* and *Roe* had been in their time. If the Court upholds the Florida Act, he fears that pro-elderly legislation at the expense of the education of youth will eventually sweep the country. Depending on how the Court chooses to strike down the Florida Act, a variety of results is possible. At times, he wishes that he still had the support of all of the Justices for finally determining under the fifth, ninth, and fourteenth amendments that deprivation of virtually all publicly supported education after the age of fourteen is unconstitutional, now and forever. But as he looks back at the history of judicial review, he realizes that no Court really ever had that final authority to issue such fiats anyway. Even *Plessy* and *Lochner* had finally fallen by the wayside, as had *Roe*.

His reverie is broken as one of the newer, and more liberal, members of the Court argues for remanding the case to the lower courts for review under anticaste, equal protection grounds with respect to the poor, Chicano, black, handicapped, and female plaintiffs: "If we rule on discrimination grounds, we can hamstring this regressive legislation in ways that will keep Florida from reenacting its substantive policies for a long time to come." The next-senior Justice, a conservative ideologue, counters,

> That's just like you liberals, trying to figure out how unelected Justices can best stifle the legitimate operation of the democratic process forever whenever you disagree with the public policy enacted by the people's duly elected representatives. I don't much

> like Florida's choice about allocating resources either, but I'll be damned if I'll go along with a ruling that plaintiffs and their counsel never even made, let alone proved.

This Justice continues lecturing his junior colleague,

> You can't act as the keeper of the holy grail for the future of the country, no matter how much wiser you think you are than the Florida legislature. Who knows, maybe you'll be surprised. Other states, or even the Congress acting on behalf of the entire country, may reject Florida's choice. Or maybe Florida will surprise all of us: maybe its concentration of resources on the talented fifth will lead to a new revolution that will allow the country to regain our position of economic and moral leadership in the world. Or maybe the 80 percent of Florida youth who are barred from the state's college prep schools will lead a political revolution that will reawaken the country to the need for more fundamental reforms in public schooling. Or maybe those of the 80 percent who can afford to pay for vocational training or join Florida's job corps will prove to be the entrepreneurs and workers who can compete. Or maybe the people of Florida have really seen the future: perhaps, all we can really hope to do is provide as fulfilling a retirement as possible for our elderly population, while the country as a whole enters its own old age and retirement in the ongoing world economic struggle. We can't know for sure what is right. Why don't we give the political process of the State of Florida, and of the other states, a chance to work?

At this point the respected woman Justice whose vote had formed the majorities on the Court to overturn *Roe* and to uphold the 1992 Pro-Life, Pro-Mother Act speaks:

> As you know, I agree that this Court should give the political process a chance to work. That's why I have consistently stuck by my provisional structure for judicial review. I think this is one of those cases in which we have an issue of such unique national importance under the Constitution that we have to make the people reflect very carefully, and through the national political process, before reallocating resources from the education of juveniles to the care of the elderly. Education of young people in this country isn't just another public good, like recreation, housing, or health care. This Court has repeatedly said as much from *Brown* to *Plyler*. Remember, even Justice Powell, who was very chary about declaring education a constitutional right, joined the Court's judgment in *Plyler*.

This Florida Act threatens the very future of the country. It's not an isolated aberration. I fear that if we uphold the Florida Act, similar legislation is likely to sweep the country just as Jim Crow laws did after the Court's approval of separate but equal in *Plessy*. The dissatisfaction with the public schools, coupled with the interstate power of big business to demand that other states match Florida's cut in taxes and with the power of the elderly to demand similar services, will likely prevail unless we step in now with all of our moral authority and require reconsideration of the issue through the national political process. I can't say that our view will, or even should, ultimately prevail in this national debate, but it is certainly better than giving our tacit support to the Florida Act by holding that it doesn't violate any privilege or immunity of these plaintiff children who, after all, are still citizens of this country.

The next-senior member of the Court follows:

If we strike down this Act now and promote a national political debate, the stakes will go way up. I'd rather uphold this Florida Act as rational legislation about whose costs and benefits we express no view, than make this another test case for your still-novel theory of provisional review. Your approach may have carried the day in overturning *Roe* and upholding the Pro-Life, Pro-Mother Act of 1992 because you held the swing vote, but I'm not sure that we ought to use that approach to create new rights in the area of public education. We all know that *Brown* and *Plyler* were really cases about caste subjugation, not about education per se. We've never held that education of our young people is any kind of constitutional right. If we so hold under your theory of provisional review, the Congress may just come back and enact legislation under the commerce clause telling all of the states to adopt something like what Florida has done. If you are right about the political climate, the power of big business and the self-interest of the growing elderly population, then watch out.

This Justice continues,

Or maybe we should just say that we were wrong to grant review in this case. That will mean that the judgment of the court of appeals stands, but we don't have to issue any opinion. Then, Florida's Act will fall, and the district judge will begin to frame some kind of remedy. God help her in that monumental task. I'm sure that these eight plaintiffs will have long since reached their full maturity before any injunction issues. I hate to admit it, but I hope that the trial judge takes a long time before ordering any remedy. In the meantime, maybe the political climate will change before 80 percent of another generation of children is lost in Florida or in any other state.

After listening to the other Justices, the Chief Justice speaks quietly:

It's obvious this is a hard case. Neither the Constitution nor the framers' intent provides the answer. They don't tell us the answer to the question on which we ordered reargument: is publicly supported education a privilege or immunity of national citizenship and, if so, to what extent? We have to make that tough choice for ourselves. And, for better or worse, I won't ask you to revisit the rationale for this Court's holdings in the cases overturning *Roe* and upholding the Pro-Life, Pro-Mother Act of 1992 by arguing that the privileges or immunities clause is really just a dead letter after all.

Whatever we decide on the merits of the basic issue before us, our choice in this case may prove crucial for at least a generation to come. I don't hear anyone who thinks the Florida Act makes for good public policy. But bad policy is not a sufficient reason to strike down any state act, no matter how wrongheaded we may think it is.

Turning to the junior Justice, the Chief Justice advises,

I do, however, share many of the concerns and fears that all of you have spoken about this Florida Act. It might have been convenient for us if the plaintiffs had brought this case as some kind of discrimination claim on behalf of discrete classes who may continue to be relegated to a second-class status by the thoughtlessness of the Florida legislature. But the plaintiffs didn't try the case on that basis, and we'd look foolish now if we based our ruling on any anticaste principle. The most that we should do in that regard is issue a little warning, to suggest in a footnote or two that equal protection issues, which *may* be raised by others who might challenge such acts in the future, are not before us in this case. Indeed, even if we remanded this case for consideration of the discrimination issues, I'm not sure that we'd really be dealing with what this case is about. I can envision all kinds of responses by the Florida legislature that might affirmatively protect every insular minority that we can imagine, but still deprive the vast majority of Florida's children who don't make the "talented fifth" of all meaningful educational opportunity supported by the state after age fourteen.

Pausing for emphasis, the Chief Justice continues,

On the other hand, I do think that we can play an important role in shaping the public debate on the basic constitutional issue raised by the Florida Act. This case is ripe for decision. If we choose to duck the issue now, then we will have defaulted in our obligation to tell the people what we think the privileges or immunities clause means in contemporary America, just as surely as if we were to hold that the clause is a dead letter.

We can't know with certainty whether the people will agree with our reading, nor precisely how their representatives in Congress will react to any ruling that we might make. Nevertheless, I think this case raises constitutional issues of enduring significance. We are at a watershed. However we rule, the case will be a landmark for better or worse. In my mind the issue for decision is this: are juveniles, ages fifteen through seventeen, entitled at this time to a state-supported education as one of the opportunities so essential to being a member of the national community that the State of Florida must make it available?

With a bow to his respected woman colleague, the Chief Justice adds,

As you know, I have had my doubts about the framework for provisional review which results from ruling on this issue under the privileges or immunities clause. It invites us to create new constitutional rights that bind the states, while allowing Congress to legislate a different result if it disagrees with our substantive judgment. Both aspects of this approach are troubling to me. But it does have particular merit in this case. I think we all believe this Florida Act, if it sweeps the country, is likely to deprive the nation of the development of its most precious resource, the potential of our young people if nurtured by a decent education. None of us wants to be a party to such probable devastation if we can help it. If we were to uphold the Act on the ground that it is rational or determine that there is no right to education in the circumstances of this case, we will inevitably encourage the enactment of such state legislation. We ought to have learned that much from the sorry history of the country following *Plessy*. On the other hand, if we think that we have the final power to tell the people that they have to provide secondary schooling for young people rather than health care, recreation, and housing for the elderly, we are fooling ourselves. Provisional review gives us a way to strike down the Florida Act without claiming a power that we do not in practice hold.

Addressing his conservative brethren, the Chief Justice counsels,

> But these institutional and policy issues are not the real reason that I believe the Florida Act violates the privileges or immunities clause of the fourteenth amendment. Chief Justice Warren may have generated much criticism from all of the pointy-headed commentators when he focused his ruling in *Brown* on the impact of segregation on the black children who were the victims of that caste subjugation. And he surely made a mistake when he cited psychological studies to support his ruling. But he ultimately hit a sympathetic chord, both with the Constitution and with the American people, when he found that black schoolchildren were hurt in their hearts and minds in a way unlikely ever to be undone by the caste system of Jim Crow segregation. I think we need to focus our judgment, and our opinion, on these eight young people who are the plaintiffs in this case. For each of them, the Florida Act disables them, in one way or another, from being able to aspire to what it means, in this day and age, to be a full citizen in these United States.
>
> For some, the Florida Act disables them from gaining the rudimentary communication skills necessary to exercise their rights of speech and of participation in the political process, which the Constitution guarantees to assure the effective functioning of our representative democracy. For others, the ability to become self-reliant and self-sufficient citizens will be forever lost. Still others will be deprived of the basic tools necessary to lead productive economic lives. Several are denied access to the building block of secondary education necessary to allow them even to aspire to higher education. All are denied the educational opportunity, without which it is doubtful that any may reasonably be expected to succeed in life. I don't believe the Florida Act provides those conditions to which these eight plaintiff children are entitled in this day and age by virtue of their citizenship in these United States.
>
> In so holding, we don't need to denigrate the interests of the elderly in decent housing, recreation, and health care, nor the interests of business and other taxpayers in lower taxes. Our ruling must leave the Florida legislature with discretion to decide such issues, to retain the tax cut *and* the new system of retirement boards. Nor do we have to compel Florida to go back to its former K–12 system of public schooling. Certainly, the dissatisfaction with the public school systems of this country cannot be gainsaid. What form public support for the education of juveniles may take under our ruling should remain up to the State of Florida.

> I realize that the framers of the fourteenth amendment never contemplated that public education was any kind of privilege or immunity. But Chief Justice Warren had it right there too. We need to examine the issue in light of today's prevailing circumstances, not what existed in 1868. The framers could not predict the future. That's why they chose general language capable of growth over time. It is enough for now if we hold that education is the very foundation of citizenship in this day and age.
>
> We can leave for another day what are the other privileges or immunities of national citizenship. I don't even want to begin to hint that there is anything else. Let another Court, at another time, grapple with the limits of the privileges or immunities clause. It's enough to note that we won't create a slippery slope that includes all claims for substantive entitlements by ruling in favor of the claim of these eight plaintiffs to some meaningful, publicly supported secondary education this day.

Satisfied that he has the attention if not the agreement of all of the Justices to this point, the Chief proceeds,

> That leaves the issue of remedy. In this case, we are somewhat more fortunate than in *Brown*. This is not a class action, and we do not address a system of segregation by which an entrenched white in-group seeks to subjugate all blacks as an outcast group. Our ruling on remedy can therefore be narrowly tailored to permit immediate relief for the eight plaintiffs before us.
>
> First, we should declare the Florida Act unconstitutional as a violation of what it means for each of these eight children to be a citizen of these United States under the fourteenth amendment.
>
> Second, we should remand to the district court for hearings on framing compensatory relief forthwith for each of the eight plaintiffs. Unlike the much more difficult situation faced by the Court in *Brown,* there is no reason to delay the framing of relief for these plaintiffs while Florida sorts out what it wants to do about supporting postelementary education generally.
>
> Third, we should instruct the district judge not to enjoin Florida to reinstate its old K–12 system of public schooling. Who knows, maybe our ruling will inspire the people of Florida to come up with something better now that we have held that the state can't just shunt most of its fifteen-year-olds into the streets, a job corps, or a proprietary vocational school.
>
> Fourth, I will even go along with a strong hint that our ruling need not be retroactive with respect to the many teenagers in Florida who may have been or will be deprived of their right to

> postelementary education under our reading of the privileges of national citizenship under the fourteenth amendment. Although countless children may thereby forever lose their opportunity for judicial relief, maybe we as a Court should not hold the State of Florida responsible after the fact for failing to forsee how we choose today to infuse the Constitution with new meaning by our interpretation of the privileges or immunities clause. By declaring the basic right to education without ordering complete relief for the children excluded from publicly supported education who are not plaintiffs in this case, we will leave the basic tension of unremedied wrongs for resolution by the political process in the first instance. Don't be surprised if Congress or the State of Florida is moved to provide some form of relief for all of these children if the country accepts our declaration that the opportunity of a decent education after the age of fourteen is a national right. Unlike the situation facing the country in *Brown,* in which a dominant majority could not be trusted to remedy its systematic subjugation of an insular minority, we should place more faith in the political process voluntarily to promote workable and effective remedies for violation of substantive rights affecting a much broader segment of our population. If the people come to accept education as a basic national right, you'll be surprised at how complete, even innovative the remedial responses may be.
>
> Finally, we should warn the district judge against enjoining Florida's new system of retirement boards and tax cuts. Our declaration of education as a national privilege can be a clarion call and our command of relief for these eight plaintiffs can be immediate. But we should not tell Florida how to allocate its resources between various governmental services, how to raise revenues, or how to take care of the elderly.

Pausing to allow the other Justices time to reflect, the Chief Justice notes,

> That brings us to the final question: how will the people and their elected representatives in Congress respond to our ruling? I can't claim to know the answer. I will say this: By focusing our opinion on what we believe the privileges or immunities clause means for each of these eight young people as citizens of the United States today, we will at least make our most honest, and persuasive, statement to the American people. We can thereby shape the terms of the resulting national debate over what it means to be a member of the national community under our Constitution.

Sounding a rueful note, the Chief Justice concludes,

> Whatever my personal wishes and hopes, I am prepared, finally, to join the majority of you in agreeing that provisional review has some merit when we deal with substantive rights. We can declare what we think the privileges or immunities clause means. But, in the end, this Court does not and, in retrospect, never has finally controlled the ultimate outcome of the ongoing national dialogue over the substantive meaning of the Constitution.

Following the Chief Justice's lead, the Justices vote unanimously to hold that the Florida Act violates the privileges or immunities of the eight plaintiffs as citizens under the fourteenth amendment. Thereafter, all join in the Chief Justice's frank opinion. Within sixty days, the eight plaintiffs and the State of Florida agree to a settlement whereby the state provides tuition for the children for one extra year of education beyond the age of eighteen, at an educational institution to be agreed upon by the individual child and the state, for each year between the ages of fifteen and eighteen that they have previously been deprived of state-supported education.

Imagine that Congress responds within a year by enacting a "National Personal Development Trust Act" (NPDTA). The NPDTA is passed pursuant to the spending and commerce clause in view of the impact that the opportunity of education and training for a lifetime has on the general welfare and commerce of the nation. It is also passed pursuant to section 5 of the fourteenth amendment to enforce by appropriate legislation the rights guaranteed in section one.

The preamble to the Act states,

> Based on testimony on the Court's ruling, the Congress finds that education and training are of critical importance to the growth of the individual and to the survival of the republic. The Court's opinion serves to remind the entire nation what it means to be a citizen of these United States. No matter how pressing the alternative needs of the moment may appear, we as a nation cannot deprive our young people of all meaningful educational opportunity after the age of fourteen. Without the opportunity for a decent education, no person can reasonably be expected to succeed in life nor to enjoy the blessings of liberty that our Constitution guarantees for all. Without educating each succeeding generation, no nation committed to democratic self-government can be expected to long endure nor to enjoy the benefits of prosperity. All of our young people are entitled to education and training in the years ahead, and any person who has been denied the opportunity of meaningful education and training prior to the age of eighteen is entitled to a remedy.

The preamble continues,

> This does not, however, mean that the nation must continue forever to use the traditional K–12 system of state-supported public schooling to provide this national privilege of citizenship. We face new challenges and new opportunities today. Indeed, rapid technological change and increasing world-wide competition compel us to provide the opportunity of education and training for life if our people and our industry are to prosper in the years ahead. But we cannot finance such a lifetime system of education and training with public taxes, nor offer meaningful educational opportunity to all ages by expanding our elementary and secondary schools. Instead, the Congress has determined that a self-sustaining, national trust fund should be created to provide all persons after the age of fifteen with a means to *invest* in their own education. This National Personal Development Trust will encourage *all* persons after the age of fifteen to invest their own time in educating themselves in exchange for repaying thereafter a portion of the resulting economic benefit.

The preamble adds,

> Our hearings also demonstrate that we must broaden the basic public education that the states *must* provide to our children prior to the age of sixteen. In addition to learning math, English, and computers, it is critical that our citizenry study the history of our country and its place in the history of the world, as well as the wonders of science, the arts, and languages and cultures foreign to our own.

The preamble concludes,

> The states of course are free, as most now do, to provide more support for secondary schooling and higher education. The NPDTA is designed to provide a foundation for a new system of education and training for life, and it imposes no ceiling on any state's own initiatives and investment in their constituents' schooling nor on any family's support for more education, public or private, for their own children. The NPDTA will encourage all of our people, and all of the states, to invest in the future of our citizens. By building on the self-interest of each person in investing in his or her own education and training at any time in life, we promote the common good of all our people and the general welfare of the entire nation.

Imagine further that the hypothetical NPDTA's substantive provisions require, first, that each state make available a specified minimum of public schooling for all children through the age of fifteen. In addition to basic skills training in math, English, and computer literacy, the NPDTA requires the states to provide training in the arts, music, foreign languages, physical fitness, American history and culture, world history, and science. The NPDTA authorizes the states to provide such schooling through state funding of tuition vouchers for accredited nonreligious schools given to each family, state decentralization of the responsibility to local school districts, or any other organizational structure that the states can invent.

Second, for all persons from the age of sixteen through their death, the NPDTA creates a self-sustaining, national trust fund for education, training, and personal development. This trust fund allows any individual to obtain additional years of schooling at any institution of learning or training to which he or she is accepted that has been accredited by a state and the Secretary of Education or by accreditation services approved by any state and the Secretary. Tuition payments are made directly from the trust fund on behalf of the recipient to the provider of the service. The NPDTA authorizes the Secretary to deny accreditation to any institution or program that discriminates on grounds of race, sex, national origin, age, wealth, or participation in the trust. The Secretary is also authorized to withhold or to revoke accreditation to any provider of educational service that fails to provide meaningful education or training opportunities commensurate with the tuition charged by the provider.

Third, in exchange for each year of tuition for schooling or training after the age of seventeen, the Act compels the recipient to pay back to the trust the greater of 2 percent per year of his or her income or wealth for life. For persons who choose to take a part-time course of instruction or training, the 2 percent per year repayment is reduced accordingly. The NPDTA makes this repayment of the trust's investment in the person's education or training deductible from the gross income of the individual under both federal and state income taxes and a credit against federal and state inheritance taxes. Eligibility for tuition payments is limited after age twenty-one to five years in any ten-year period, except that persons who serve in the armed forces, the Peace Corps, Vista, or other community services approved by the President are eligible for two additional years of tuition from the fund for each year of such public service.

Finally, the NPDTA provides that each person who has previously been denied the opportunity of a publicly supported education prior to the age of eighteen by any state may receive tuition for one extra year for each year denied a publicly supported education without having to make any repayment to the trust.

In response to the Court's ruling and the NPDTA, imagine also that Florida amends its Retirement-Vocation-Education Priority Act to limit its exclusion from state-supported education to children sixteen and over and to limit the state college prep schools for the talented fifth to grades ten through twelve. The amendment also provides for state funding of vouchers for the education of children after the fifth grade through the age of fifteen at any nonreligious school. Finally, the amendment supplies tuition vouchers for one extra year of schooling for each year a child has previously been denied state support for education prior to the age of sixteen.

Assuming that there is no defect in the process by which Congress legislates the NPDTA or by Florida in its enactment or operation of its amended Act, there should be little doubt that a Court committed to provisional review would find no constitutional violation in either Act.* As we have seen throughout the discussion of four types of cases in Part II, provisional review authorizes the Court to initiate and to shape a national dialogue over what substantive rights we as a people choose to interpret from the Constitution. Ultimately, however, the Court does not have the final say.

Upon review of a lower court's judgment in an appropriate case or controversy, a Court committed to provisional review would uphold both Acts. Imagine a brief opinion signed individually by each of the nine Justices that reads as follows:

> We welcome the legislative responses of the Congress and of the State of Florida to our ruling holding that education is a national privilege under section 1 of the fourteenth amendment. Congress has broad discretion in exercising its enumerated powers in declaring and implementing national policies, including those relating to fundamental rights of national citizenship. Finding no constitutional violation in the process of enacting the National Personal Development Trust Act, we hold that this act is a valid exercise of the legislative power vested in Congress by the Constitution. Similarly, we find that Florida's amendments to its prior Act do not conflict with the Constitution nor with the NPDTA. To the contrary, when coupled with the NPDTA, the Florida amendments provide appropriate means to implement the national privilege of education for the people of Florida.

Once again, the point of this hypothetical case is to illustrate how provisional review could work to assist the Court in promoting an ongoing dialogue over what it means to be a member of the national community. Initially, the Court declares a national right as against the states, here a right to education under the privileges or immunities clause of the four-

*In the alternative, of course, Congress might enact its own National Retirement-Vocation-Education Priority Act modeled after the Florida statute. Or Congress could instead authorize the states to exercise their own legislative discretion to develop their own priority acts, to stick with their current systems of elementary and secondary public schooling, or to provide incentives for state secondary and higher education tuition trust funds.

teenth amendment against the State of Florida. The Court's ruling posits a point of view on an issue of vital national importance. This, in turn, promotes a dialogue with the people over the nature and importance of the asserted national right. The people, through their representatives in Congress, may then respond with appropriate national legislation enforcing, modifying, or rescinding the national right asserted by the Court; or the Congress may simply authorize the states to come up with their own answers to the issue.

As we have seen in the diverse free speech, race, and personhood hypotheticals discussed in the preceding chapters, the Court is not without power to shape this ongoing national dialogue. First, the Court may exercise all of its institutional prestige and the power of its uniquely public rulings to influence the outcome when it first posits a national right. Second, the Court can assure that the process of congressional lawmaking is representative, open, and actually focuses on the merits of the issue. Third, the Court can make sure that the Congress is not influenced by the wishes of the majority simply to subordinate an unpopular minority to a second-class citizenship. Under provisional review, therefore, the Court would have a unique opportunity to promote an ongoing dialogue over the meaning of the Constitution.

Whether provisional review would encourage a future Court to declare education—or any other service, benefit, or opportunity—a privilege of membership in these United States cannot be predicted with any certainty. Provisional review, however, does empower the Court to make such a declaration. At the same time, we the people would retain the power under provisional review to enact a different answer through national legislation. Provisional review therefore makes clear that the Court's authority depends, ultimately, on the wisdom of the choices it makes in interpreting the meaning of the Constitution, not on any claim that the Court's word is final.

NOTES

1. Brown v. Bd. of Educ., 347 U.S. 483, 493–94 (1954).
2. *See* discussion chapters 1 and 5 *supra*.
3. San Antonio Independent School District v. Rodriguez, 411 U.S. 1, 30 (1973).
4. 411 U.S. at 33.
5. 411 U.S. at 33–34.
6. 411 U.S. at 35. To plaintiffs' argument that education should nevertheless be viewed as a fundamental personal right under the Constitution because essential for the exercise of the basic constitutional rights of speech and voting, Powell responded that there was no indication that the state school finance system "occasioned an absolute denial of educational opportunities to any of its children. . . . [N]o charge fairly could be made that the system fails to provide each child with an oppor-

tunity to acquire the basic minimal skills necessary for the enjoyment of the rights of speech and of full participation in the political process." San Antonio Independent School District v. Rodriguez, 411 U.S. 1, 36–37 (1973). Justice Powell added that if "some identifiable quantum of education is a constitutionally protected prerequisite to the meaningful exercise of either right [,] . . . [e]mpirical examination might well buttress an assumption that the ill-fed, ill-clothed, and ill-housed are the most ineffective participants in the political process and they derive the least enjoyment from the benefits of the First Amendment." *Id.*

7. *See* R. KLUGER, SIMPLE JUSTICE (1976) for a revealing history of the school segregation cases. To understand the nature of the fiscal discrimination at issue in the state school finance cases, *see, e.g.*, J. COONS, et al., PRIVATE WEALTH AND PUBLIC EDUCATION 20–21 (1970); P. DIMOND, A DILEMMA OF LOCAL GOVERNMENT: DISCRIMINATION IN THE PROVISION OF PUBLIC SERVICES 20–21 (1978); and Dimond, *Serrano,* 2 YALE REV. OF L. & SOC. ACTION 133 (1973).
8. San Antonio Independent School District v. Rodriguez, 411 U.S. at 25–28. In Kadrmas v. Dickinson Public Schools, 101 L.Ed2d 399 (1988), the Court in a narrow 5 to 4 ruling upheld a local school district's charging fees to families for transporting their children to school. The majority reiterated that education is *not* a "fundamental right, . . . which should trigger strict scrutiny when government interferes with an individual's access to it."
9. *Id.* The Court has been just as unsympathetic to a variety of claims of exclusionary zoning, even where racial implications boil under the surface of the fiscal and wealth discrimination. *See* James v. Valtierra, 402 U.S. 137 (1971); Warth v. Seldin, 422 U.S. 490 (1975); and Village of Arlington Heights v. M.H.D.C., 429 U.S. 252 (1977).
10. Plyler v. Doe, 457 U.S. 202 (1982).
11. 457 U.S. at 219, 230, 234, 241.
12. L. TRIBE, AMERICAN CONSTITUTIONAL LAW 1552 (1988).

CONCLUSION

Provisional Review as a Judicial Choice: Preserving the Voice of the Court while Assuring the Consent of the People

Provisional review exposes the twin myths of the traditional theory of judicial review. First, the Justices in interpreting the Constitution do not always find specific answers provided by the text and the framers' intent; instead, the Court must often make its own law by choosing among the range of alternatives authorized by the Constitution. Second, the Court's interpretations of the Constitution usually do not provide the final word as to its substantive meaning; instead, the Court's decisions begin an ongoing national dialogue over the meaning of the Constitution and shape the process by which we the people choose to govern ourselves.

To date, the Court has not expressly embraced the structure of provisional review as elaborated here. Perhaps this is because the twin myths of the traditional theory of judicial review serve to protect the Court's judgments for some time from opposition by a people generally committed to the rule of law. Indeed, if the people or their representatives in Congress ever come to understand that the Court's decisions are in any part judge-made choices that begin rather than end public debate over the meaning of the Constitution, there may be a risk that they may disregard the Court's interpretation altogether as just another policy-making voice.

Yet when the history of the Supreme Court is viewed from the perspective of generations, there is no mistaking that the Court's judgments have been provisional in fact. Even if a Court has claimed that one interpretation or another was compelled by the text or framers' intent and that its interpretation represented the final word, the meaning of the Constitution *has* changed over time. Whether by constitutional amendment, changes in the Court's personnel, shifts in the national mood, judicial responses to an onslaught of conflicting national and state legislation, or evolution in the Court's own thinking, the meaning of the Constitution has not been constant, and it has not been dictated by the framers' intent.[1]

The framers of the Constitution refused to give specific answers to the questions raised in most hard cases that come before the Court. Instead, the framers chose general language, capable of growth and evolution, in drafting most of the controversial provisions of the Constitution. As a result, the Court's answers are not final but are inevitably subject to change as the Court makes hard choices in interpreting the meaning of the Constitution over time.

This understanding of the historic reality exposes the conflict of judicial review with representative democracy. An unelected Court inevitably must make constitutional law, either by substituting its judgment for the laws enacted by the people's duly elected representatives in the states and in Congress or by validating the policies enacted by the legislatures. Provisional review resolves this conflict, first, by giving Congress the power to override through ordinary legislation the Court's interpretation of most national rights that bind the states and, second, by limiting judicial review of such national laws generally to the process of lawmaking, except with respect to a surprisingly few substantive values enumerated in the Bill of Rights. Thus, provisional review provides a structure for judicial interpretation of the Constitution that is consistent with the nation's commitment to representative democracy.

Provisional review provides this alternative framework for judicial review by choosing to interpret the meaning of the Constitution *within* the range of choices authorized by the text, framing, and ratification of the Constitution. It allows the Court to continue its vital role, both in interpreting individual rights under the fourteenth amendment that the states must respect and in shaping the resulting national dialogue by reviewing the national law-making process to assure that it is representative and open, free from caste-based defects, and clearly focused on the merits of the issues for decision. It is consistent with the federal structure of the United States and with the traditional roles of the states, the Congress, and the Court in resolving federal-state conflicts. Finally, it preserves the voice of the Court on the full range of substantive, procedural, separation of power, and federalism issues raised in the Constitution, while ultimately assuring the consent of the people through their representatives in Congress.

Provisional review, of course, entails many risks of its own. When the nation most needs a strong Court under provisional review to assure that the process of lawmaking is not tainted by caste or that unpopular voices of the moment are not outlawed, there is always the possibility that a weak Court will just rationalize caste subjugation or find that the current threat to government justifies those in power silencing the dangerous message. But this is also a risk for a Court that claims to find final answers in the framers' intent with respect to the process of lawmaking. Or when the nation most needs an independent voice of reason to assist in evaluating a conflict between state coercion and personal autonomy, there is always a risk that a Court fearful of congressional override under provisional review will just duck the issue. But this is also a risk for a Court that claims to find final answers to such substantive questions in interpreting the meaning of the Constitution by arguing that the framers either did not address the issue at all or decided it, one way or the other, once and for all.

Provisional review provides a lens through which to examine how the nation lives with the apparent tension between judicial review and representative democracy under a Constitution that the framers wrote in general terms so that future generations would have the opportunity to make their own choices about its meanings. Ultimately, we the people consent to judicial review: either we come to accept the content of the Court's current interpretations; *or* the content of the constitutional law changes over time, whether by amendment or shifts in the composition or thinking of the Court, to fit the will of the people. This process *is* an ongoing dialogue between the Court and the people over the meaning of the Constitution. In sum, provisional review provides a paradigm of how this dialogue may proceed consistent with representative democracy under our federal system. It shows, finally, why we the people should be more concerned about the meaning we choose to read into the Constitution than arguing about whether the Court's interpretations are compelled by the framers' intent or are final. In the words of Harry Wellington, "We the people consent" to judicial review, because, "in one fashion or another, we have adequate control over the content of the law that governs us."[2]

In the years ahead, it is therefore not necessary for the Court to embrace all aspects of provisional review at once. It may be wiser for the Court to begin to use the privileges or immunities clause rather than the due process clause as the source for positing substantive national rights of individuals under section 1 of the fourteenth amendment as against the states. This will allow the Court, the people, and Congress to explore how the national dialogue over the meaning of the Constitution should proceed. Whether provisional review is thereafter expressly embraced by reading the Bill of Rights generally to shape the process of national lawmaking or a more flexible framework evolves to permit the Court to review the substance of national laws in selective areas under the ninth amendment, both the people and the Court will know that judicial interpretations will remain final only so long as they gain the consent of the people over time. In either case, the voice of the Court will continue to be heard so long as the Court continues to speak and its rulings help the people take a closer look at the merits of the constitutional principles at issue.

The Court, the commentators, and the people in time will come to recognize the inevitability of judicial choice in interpreting the meaning of the Constitution. When that happens, there will no longer be any respectable claim that the Court's judgments should be final because specifically intended by the framers or directly compelled by the text of the Constitution. This does not mean that the constitutional text, history of framing, or prior judicial precedent are irrelevant to any Justice's vote or to the persuasive power of her opinions. To the contrary, these sources do serve, in the words of former Solicitor General Archibald Cox, as a "confining force" in the process of constitutional adjudication. But these sources do not compel a single answer to many questions that confront the Court. In these hard cases, judicial review by the Court inevitably takes on a "creative aspect" in interpreting the meaning of the Constitution.[3]

The Court's ultimate influence will therefore depend in the future, as it really has in the past, on the independence, integrity, wisdom, and insight of its rulings in interpreting the meaning of the Constitution. That may place an awesome burden of responsibility on each Justice in choosing how to decide the hard cases that come before the Court, but it eliminates the spectre of a few unelected judicial oracles joining to form a radical or reactionary Court to control finally the destiny of the country for generations to come.

NOTES

1. As examples, consider: the fourteenth amendment's revision of the Court's earlier judgment that no black person could be a citizen of the United States (*see* discussion *supra,* Introduction, text at note 19, and chapter 1, text at note 35); the Modern Court's rejection of the state sovereignty limits on congressional power under the commerce clause imposed in Hammer v. Dagenhart (chapter 2, note 17); the Modern Court's rejection of active review of economic and social welfare legislation under a substantive reading of the due process clause imposed during the *Lochner* era (Introduction, note 49 and text at notes 20–22, and chapter 2, at notes 17 and 24); the Warren Court's reversal of the *Plessy* Court's rationale for forced segregation of the races (Introduction, notes 3 and 5, and chapter 1, text at notes 1–31); and the development by the Modern Court of a variety of substantive and representation-reinforcing values as national rights of the individual under section 1 of the fourteenth amendment despite the *Slaughter-house* Court's restrictive view of the meaning of this provision (Introduction, text at note 17 and note 63; chapter 2, text at notes 38–43 and note 40; chapter 4, at note 5). Nor do these changes in the meaning of the Constitution always take generations. For example, the reversal of Justice Rehnquist's attempt to reinvoke state sovereignty limits on congressional power took less than a decade on the Burger Court (*see* discussion chapter 2 *supra,* note 17). But that is not even close to the record: in the compulsory flag salute cases, the Court rejected its previous interpretation of the meaning of the Constitution in *three* years. *Compare* West Virginia State Bd. of Educ. v. Barnette, 319 U.S. 624 (1943) *with* Minersville School Dist. v. Gobitis, 310 U.S. 586 (1940).
2. Wellington, *Book Review,* 97 HARV. L. REV. 326, 335 (1983).
3. *See* A. COX, THE COURT AND THE CONSTITUTION 377 (1987).

Index